ACTION!
CARTOONING

WRITTEN AND
ILLUSTRATED BY
BEN CALDWELL

96 PAGES
OF HOW-TO
HAVOC!

STERLING PUBLISHING CO., INC.
NEW YORK

LIBRARY OF
CONGRESS CATALOGING-IN-
PUBLICATION DATA AVAILABLE

2 4 6 8 10 9 7 5 3 1

PUBLISHED BY STERLING PUBLISHING CO., INC.
387 PARK AVENUE SOUTH, NEW YORK, NY 10016
© 2004 BY BEN CALDWELL
DISTRIBUTED IN CANADA BY STERLING PUBLISHING
C/O CANADIAN MANDA GROUP, ONE ATLANTIC AVENUE, SUITE 105
TORONTO, ONTARIO, CANADA M6K 3E7
DISTRIBUTED IN GREAT BRITAIN AND EUROPE BY CHRIS LLOYD AT ORCA BOOK
SERVICES, STANLEY HOUSE, FLEETS LANE, POOLE BH15 3AJ, ENGLAND
DISTRIBUTED IN AUSTRALIA BY CAPRICORN LINK (AUSTRALIA) PTY. LTD.
P.O. BOX 704, WINDSOR, NSW 2756, AUSTRALIA

PRINTED IN CHINA

STERLING ISBN 1-4027-1462-9

CONTENTS

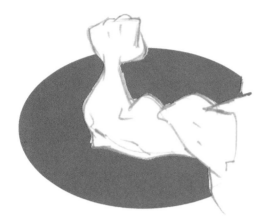

THE BASICS!

OBVIOUSLY, IF YOU'RE LOOKING AT THIS BOOK, YOU'RE INTERESTED IN DRAWING CARTOONS. JOIN THE CLUB! BUT THIS BOOK ISN'T JUST STEP-BY-STEP INSTRUCTIONS -- IT SHOWS HOW THE PARTS OF THE BODY AND THE FACE FIT TOGETHER, AND HOW YOU CAN ALTER THEM TO CREATE UNIQUE CHARACTERS AND POSES. PERHAPS MOST IMPORTANT, THIS BOOK WILL SHOW YOU SOME OF THE TRICKS AND IDEAS YOU CAN USE TO MAKE YOUR PICTURES CONVEY JUST THE RIGHT PERSONALITIES, ACTIONS, AND MOODS YOU HAVE IN MIND!

INTRODUCTION

LET'S TALK DRAWING! CARTOONING IS NOT JUST A STYLE, IT'S AN ATTITUDE -- A COMPLETELY DIFFERENT WAY OF DRAWING REALITY. THE GOAL OF CARTOONING IS ACTION! EMOTION! YOU DON'T JUST *SEE* A CARTOON DRAWING, YOU *FEEL* IT!

THIS MEANS BOILING EVERY DRAWING DOWN TO ITS ESSENTIALS. IF A DETAIL IS IMPORTANT, EXAGGERATE IT! IF IT'S NOT IMPORTANT, SKIP IT! THAT'S WHY SO MANY CARTOONS ARE SIMPLE -- THEY NEED TO BE EASY TO READ, WITHOUT UNNECESSARY DISTRACTIONS.

BUT EVEN IMPORTANT DETAILS ALONE AREN'T AS IMPORTANT AS THE OVERALL IMPRESSION A DRAWING MAKES. *THE GREAT SECRET OF CARTOONING IS USING LINES, SHAPES, SYMBOLS, AND SO ON TO SHOW INVISIBLE IDEAS -- LIKE THE PERSONALITY OF A CHARACTER, OR THE MOOD OF A PLACE OR EVENT.*

CONSIDER THE FOLLOWING EXAMPLES...

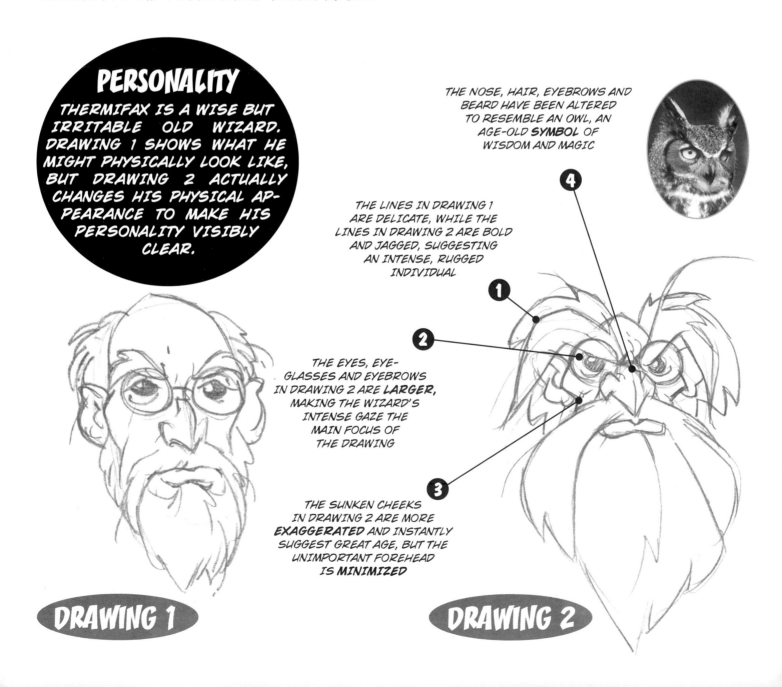

PERSONALITY

THERMIFAX IS A WISE BUT IRRITABLE OLD WIZARD. DRAWING 1 SHOWS WHAT HE MIGHT PHYSICALLY LOOK LIKE, BUT DRAWING 2 ACTUALLY CHANGES HIS PHYSICAL APPEARANCE TO MAKE HIS PERSONALITY VISIBLY CLEAR.

THE NOSE, HAIR, EYEBROWS AND BEARD HAVE BEEN ALTERED TO RESEMBLE AN OWL, AN AGE-OLD **SYMBOL** OF WISDOM AND MAGIC

THE LINES IN DRAWING 1 ARE DELICATE, WHILE THE LINES IN DRAWING 2 ARE BOLD AND JAGGED, SUGGESTING AN INTENSE, RUGGED INDIVIDUAL

THE EYES, EYE-GLASSES AND EYEBROWS IN DRAWING 2 ARE **LARGER**, MAKING THE WIZARD'S INTENSE GAZE THE MAIN FOCUS OF THE DRAWING

THE SUNKEN CHEEKS IN DRAWING 2 ARE MORE **EXAGGERATED** AND INSTANTLY SUGGEST GREAT AGE, BUT THE UNIMPORTANT FOREHEAD IS **MINIMIZED**

DRAWING 1

DRAWING 2

EMOTION

VENUS, GODDESS OF LOVE, HAS AGREED TO HELP WITH THIS EXAMPLE. YOU CAN SEE HOW BODY GESTURES AND SYMBOLS ARE A CONVENIENT, EASY TO SEE INDICATION OF AN INVISIBLE EMOTION. EVERY EMOTION HAS ITS OWN SPECIAL SIGNS.

PEOPLE CLUTCH AT THEIR HEART WHEN IT THUMPS TOO HARD -- A SURE SIGN OF UNCONTROLLABLE LOVE!

OF COURSE NO ONE EVER HAS HEARTS FLOATING AROUND HIS HEAD; THIS IS JUST A WAY FOR THE ARTIST TO SHOW US DIRECTLY WHAT THIS GUY IS THINKING

4

6

WHEN PEOPLE ARE OVERCOME WITH EMOTION, THEIR LEGS BECOME WEAK AND WOBBLY

7

PEOPLE DROOL WHEN THEY SEE SOMETHING DELICIOUS... PEOPLE ARE WEIRD!

1

5

MORE DROOL; AND A TONGUE HANGING OUT OF THE SIDE OF THE MOUTH SAYS THE SAME THING

3

THIS POOR SAP ON HIS KNEES IS NOT ONLY IN A WORSHIPFUL POSITION; BY LOOKING UP AT VENUS, HE IS SHOWING THAT SHE'S THE BOSS!

2

CLASPED HANDS USUALLY MEAN A PERSON IS EXCITED BY WHAT HE SEES, OR HE IS WORSHIPPING A HIGHER POWER. OR IN THIS CASE, BOTH

SOMETIMES AN EN-TIRE PICTURE IS ABOUT NOTHING BUT HOW A PERSON IS FEELING INSIDE. WHEN A LITTLE KID CRIES, ALL YOU GET IS SOME YELLING AND A FEW TEARS. THAT'S IT. BUT TO THE KID, IT FEELS AS IF HE'S WAILING LOUD ENOUGH TO SHAKE TOKYO, AND TORRENTS OF WATER ARE GUSHING LIKE A FIRE HYDRANT OUT OF HIS EYES. SO THAT'S EXACTLY WHAT THE CARTOONIST DRAWS.

MOOD

EXAMPLE 1

THE *DARE DETECTIVES* ARE ON THE CASE IN TRANSYLVANIA, AND MAN, THEY DON'T LOOK HAPPY! HERE ARE TWO FOREST BACKGROUNDS. BOTH SCENES HAVE GRASS, TREES AND A CASTLE. BUT THE ROUNDED LEAVES AND CURVES OF EXAMPLE 1 AREN'T GOING TO SCARE ANYONE. ON THE OTHER HAND, THE BLACKENED BRANCHES AND TOWERS IN EXAMPLE 2 LOOK LIKE THORNS AND SPIKES -- IDEAL FOR A VAMPIRE'S LAIR. YOU CAN ALWAYS ADD MENACING PROPS LIKE BATS OR A "DANGER" SIGN. BUT STARTING WITH THE RIGHT **SHAPES** WILL GUARANTEE THAT THE AUDIENCE DOESN'T JUST SEE, BUT ACTUALLY **FEELS** THE MOOD THAT YOU WANT TO CREATE.

EXAMPLE 2

MATERIALS

NOW THAT THE BASICS ARE OUT OF THE WAY, WE'RE PRETTY MUCH READY TO GO! YOU JUST NEED TO GET YOUR HANDS ON SOME DRAWING SUPPLIES...

OF COUSE, YOU NEED SOMETHING TO DRAW WITH. I USE A MECHANICAL PENCIL. YOU NEVER HAVE TO SHARPEN THEM, AND YOU CAN STICK THEM IN YOUR POCKET WITHOUT BREAKING THE POINT. BUT ANY PENCIL OR PEN YOU'RE HAPPY WITH IS FINE. NO. 2 PENCILS ARE GREAT BECAUSE THEY'RE NOT TOO HARD, NOT TOO SOFT, AND YOU CAN USE THEM ON TESTS! NON-PHOTO BLUE PENCILS ARE GOOD FOR A ROUGH UNDER-DRAWING THAT YOU CAN FINISH WITH A NORMAL PENCIL.

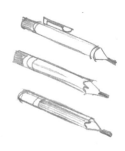

DRAWING MEANS MAKING ENDLESS MISTAKES. THAT MEANS AN ENDLESS SUPPLY OF PAPER TO RUIN. I JUST BUY REAMS (500 SHEET PACKS) OF CHEAP TYPING PAPER.

BIG MISTAKES NEED BIG ERASERS. BUY ONE. YOU SHOULD ALSO GET A GUM ERASER (THOSE CRUMBLY BROWN ONES) FOR GETTING RID OF PENCIL MARKS AFTER YOU'VE FINISHED UP A DRAWING IN INK OR MARKER.

YOUR LIBRARY, OR ANOTHER ONE NEARBY, HAS JUST ABOUT EVERY PIECE OF INFORMATION YOU COULD EVER NEED TO KNOW. WANT TO DRAW A SAMURAI? OR THE RUINS OF ANCIENT ROME? OR A GROWLING LION? I LOVE THE INTERNET, BUT NOTHING BEATS THE LOCAL LIBRARY. BY THE WAY, PICK UP AN ANATOMY BOOK FOR DETAILS ABOUT BONES AND MUSCLES. (HEY -- WE COULD ONLY FIT SO MUCH IN THIS BOOK!) MY FAVORITE IS STEPHEN PECK'S ***ATLAS OF HUMAN ANATOMY FOR THE ARTIST***.

YOU WON'T HAVE A BOOK OR EXAMPLE FOR EVERY POSE OR FACIAL EXPRESSION YOU THINK UP. SO BUY A SMALL MIRROR. IT'S EASY TO USE, EASY TO CARRY, AND CHEAPER THAN HIRING A MODEL.

AND FINALLY, YOU'LL NEED AT LEAST ONE EYE TO SEE WITH...

...A HAND TO DRAW WITH...

...AND A BRAIN TO THINK WITH -- PREFERABLY YOUR OWN!

THE FACE!

THAT'S IT FOR THE BASIC IDEAS BEHIND CARTOONING -- IT'S TIME FOR THE REAL STUFF! THE FOCUS OF ANY CHARACTER IS HIS FACE. THIS SECTION SHOWS HOW TO DRAW BASIC FACE TYPES, AND THEN MODIFY THEM TO SHOW SPECIFIC PERSONALITIES AND EMOTIONS.

FACE BASICS

YOU CAN USE THE STEP-BY-STEP INSTRUCTIONS ON THIS PAGE TO DRAW AN "AVERAGE" FACE. BUT THEY ALSO SHOW THE CONSTRUCTION OF A FACE FROM SCRATCH, AND CAN BE USED AS A ROUGH GUIDE WHEN YOU CREATE YOUR OWN, MODIFIED CARTOON FACES.

FRONT VIEW: STEP-BY-STEP

STEP 1

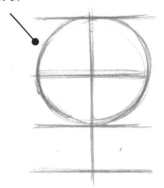

THE AVERAGE FACE IS ROUGHLY EGG-SHAPED, SO START WITH A CIRCLE DIVIDED INTO FOUR, THEN ADD A HALF CIRCLE BELOW IT

STEP 2

THE EYE LINE IS HALFWAY DOWN THE FACE, WITH ONE EYE SPACE BETWEEN THE EYES AND HALF AN EYE SPACE BETWEEN EACH EYE AND THE OUTSIDE OF THE HEAD

THE EYEBROWS ARE ABOUT THE HEIGHT OF THE CIRCLE'S HALFWAY LINE

EYELINE

NOSELINE

THE BOTTOM OF THE NOSE IS HALFWAY BETWEEN THE EYES AND CHIN. THE NOSTRILS ARE ONE EYE SPACE WIDE

STEP 3

THE HAIRLINE IS A THIRD OF THE WAY DOWN FROM THE TOP OF THE HEAD TO THE EYE LINE

THE MOUTH IS A THIRD OF THE WAY DOWN FROM THE NOSE LINE TO THE CHIN, AND IS A LITTLE WIDER THAN THE NOSTRILS

STEP 4

THE SIDES OF THE HAIRLINE COME UP AND IN FROM THE CHEEKS TO THE TOP HAIRLINE

THE CURVE OF THE UPPER CHEEK SEPARATES IT FROM THE JAW AREA

CHEEKS SLANT SLIGHTLY INWARD FROM THE EYE LINE TO THE MOUTH LINE, THEN BEND INWARD AS JAWS CONNECT TO THE CHIN, WHICH IS AS WIDE AS THE MOUTH

THE EARS COME STRAIGHT OUT FROM THE EYE LINE, THEN SLOPE DOWN TO END AT THE NOSE LINE

THE NECK IS ABOUT AS WIDE AS THE HEAD, AND SLOPES OUT AT ITS BOTTOM

PROFILE: STEP-BY-STEP

STEP 1

ANOTHER CIRCLE DIVIDED INTO QUARTERS

STEP 2

THE EAR IS LOCATED JUST BEHIND THE HALFWAY MARK, AND STRETCHES FROM EYE LINE TO NOSE LINE (THESE ARE THE SAME HEIGHT AS IN THE FRONT VIEW)

THERE IS A BROW "DENT" AT EYE LINE. THE EYE AND EYEBROW ARE JUST BEHIND IT

DRAW A LINE STRAIGHT DOWN FROM THE BROW DENT -- THIS IS THE FRONT OF THE FACE

AGAIN, THE MOUTH IS A THIRD OF THE WAY DOWN FROM NOSE TO CHIN

THE NOSE SLOPES OUT OF THE BROW DENT

STEP 3

THE CHIN PULLS STRAIGHT BACK TO THE JAW (HALF-WAY FROM THE FRONT OF THE FACE TO THE EAR LINE), SLANTS UP TO THE MOUTH LINE, AND THEN TURNS UP TO THE EAR

AT THE EYEBROW, THE FOREHEAD SLANTS UPWARD TO MEET THE HAIR LINE (A THIRD OF THE WAY FROM TOP OF HEAD TO EYE LINE) AND THE FRONT-OF-FACE LINE

THE LOWER LIP AND CHIN JUT OUT FROM THE FRONT OF THE FACE -- YOU SHOULD IMAGINE A SLANTED LINE FROM THE NOSE TIP TO THE CHIN AS A GUIDE TO HOW FAR THE UPPER AND LOWER LIP AND CHIN STICK OUT

STEP 4

THE TOP OF THE HEAD IS SLIGHTLY FLATTENED

THE NOSTRILS COME BACK TO THE FRONT OF THE EYE, AND THE LIPS COME BACK A LITTLE FURTHER

THE BASE OF THE SKULL -- JUST BELOW EYE LINE -- PULLS IN SHARPLY BEFORE IT CONNECTS TO THE NECK

FROM THE SIDE, THE NECK IS NARROWER AT THE BOTTOM THAN THE TOP

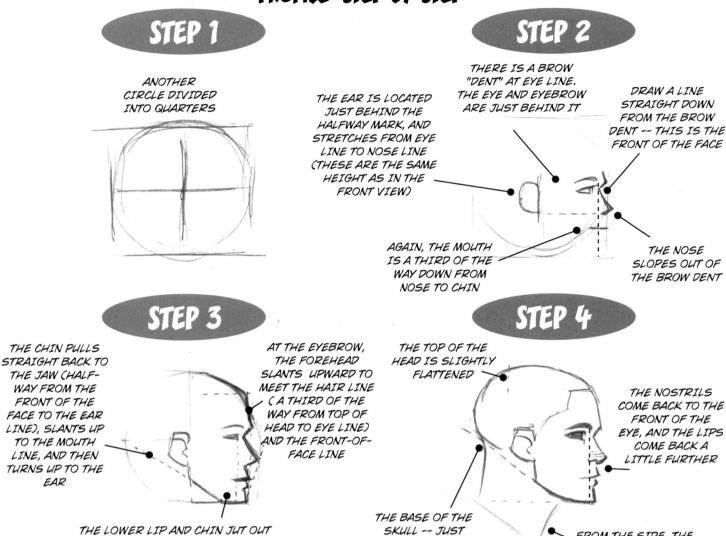

THE FEMALE FACE

THE FEMALE FACE IS MORE CURVED AND DELICATE THAN ITS MALE COUNTERPART.

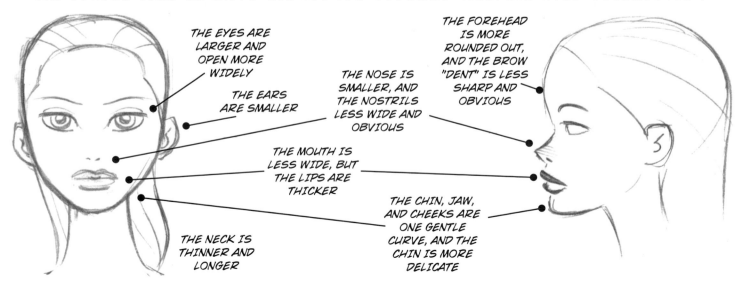

THE EYES ARE LARGER AND OPEN MORE WIDELY

THE EARS ARE SMALLER

THE NOSE IS SMALLER, AND THE NOSTRILS LESS WIDE AND OBVIOUS

THE FOREHEAD IS MORE ROUNDED OUT, AND THE BROW "DENT" IS LESS SHARP AND OBVIOUS

THE MOUTH IS LESS WIDE, BUT THE LIPS ARE THICKER

THE CHIN, JAW, AND CHEEKS ARE ONE GENTLE CURVE, AND THE CHIN IS MORE DELICATE

THE NECK IS THINNER AND LONGER

FACE PARTS

INDIVIDUAL PARTS OF THE FACE SAY AS MUCH ABOUT A CHARACTER AS THE OVERALL LOOK OF THE FACE. THERE ARE DIFFERENT "TYPES" OF EACH FACE PART, AND EACH TYPE SUGGESTS A PARTICULAR PERSONALITY OR EMOTION.

EYES

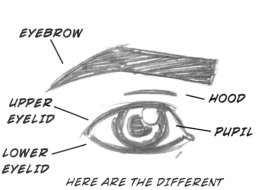

EYEBROW

UPPER EYELID

HOOD

PUPIL

LOWER EYELID

HERE ARE THE DIFFERENT PARTS OF THE EYE THAT YOU CAN ADJUST OR EXAGGERATE

IN THIS CARTOONED EYE, THE SWEEP OF THE UPPER LID IS SIMPLIFIED, WHILE THE LOWER LID IS LEFT OUT

BAD!

GOOD!

REMEMBER: IF YOU EMPHASIZE BOTH THE UPPER AND LOWER LID, THE EYE LOOKS EMOTIONLESS AND FAKE. DE-EMPHASIZE THE LOWER LID BY DRAWING IT LIGHTER (OR NOT AT ALL), AND BY MAKING THE PUPIL CLOSER TO THE UPPER LID

NO LIDS SUGGEST AN ALERT, AGGRESSIVE CHARACTER...

...WHILE AN EXAGGERATED HOOD AND FLATTENED UPPER LID HALF COVERING THE PUPIL SUGGEST A BORED OR TIRED INDIVIDUAL

TILTING THE UPPER LID AND ADDING DARK CIRCLES UNDER THE EYE SHOW LACK OF SLEEP OR ILLNESS, ES-PECIALLY WITH A SINISTER SCHEMING CHARACTER

PLACING MORE SHADING EMPHASIS ON THE UPPER LID, ESPECIALLY WHEN IT'S TILTED, CREATES A MORE SULTRY, FEMININE EXPRESSION.

SHOWING WHITE ALL AROUND THE PUPIL IS UNNATURAL -- YOU ONLY SEE THIS WHEN A CHARACTER IS SUR-PRISED OR TERRIFIED

HERE, THE EYE IS TILTED AND THE PUPIL IS PARTLY COVERED BY THE LID. THE CURVE OF THE LIDS GIVES THE EYE A MORE YOUTHFUL, INNO-CENT EXPRESSION

SHOWING WHITE ABOVE THE PUPIL (THE OPPOSITE OF MOST OF THESE EXAMPLES) COUPLED WITH CREASES IN THE LOWER LID, REVEAL A HOSTILE OR ANGRY FACE

A FLAT UPPER LID COVERED BY THE EYEBROW SHOWS A MORE RESTRAINED FORM OF HOSTILITY OR ANGER

NOSE

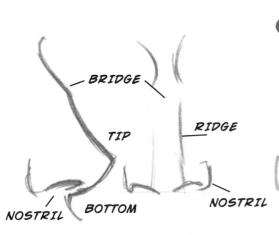

HERE ARE THE DIFFERENT PARTS OF THE NOSE THAT YOU CAN ADJUST OR EXAGGERATE

A **HAWK** OR **AQUILINE** NOSE HAS FLARING NOSTRILS AND SUGGESTS ROYALTY AND FIERCENESS. THIS IS THE NOSE OF GYPSIES, BEDOUINS, AND DRACULA!

A LONG, STRAIGHT **CLASSICAL** NOSE SHOWS NOBILITY, STRENGTH AND GRACE. THIS IS THE NOSE OF ANCIENT HEROES AND KINGS!

A **BROAD** NOSE IS A SIGN OF HONESTY, STRENGTH, AND DIGNITY. THIS IS THE NOSE OF AFRICAN PRINCES AND AZTEC WARRIORS!

A **SNUB** OR **BUTTON** NOSE SUGGESTS CUTENESS, IMPISHNESS, AND YOUTH. THIS IS THE NOSE OF PIXIES, URCHINS, AND GOOFS!

WITH ITS BENT RIDGE AND LUMPY BOTTOM, A **BROKEN** NOSE IMPLIES COARSENESS AND VIOLENCE. THIS IS THE NOSE OF STREET THUGS, BOXERS AND INNKEEPERS!

MOUTH

HERE ARE THE DIFFERENT PARTS OF THE MOUTH THAT YOU CAN ADJUST OR EXAGGERATE

A SIMPLIFIED MOUTH, WITH A SUGGESTION OF THE ORIGINAL CURVES. THE TURNED-DOWN CORNERS SHOW FIRMNESS, THE SLIGHT LOWER LIP AND NO UPPER LIP SHOW A MASCULINE CHARACTER

A FLATTER MOUTH WITH LONG DIMPLES ON THE SIDES, SHOWING A FIRM OLDER MOUTH THAT IS INCLINED TO SMILE; A STRONG, PLEASANT MOUTH

A **STANDARD FEMALE** MOUTH, WITH MORE CURVES AND AN EMPHASIZED UPPER LIP (ALTHOUGH THE LOWER LIP IS ALMOST ALWAYS FULLER.) THE CORNERS TURN UP SLIGHTLY

AN **ANGULAR** VERSION OF THE FEMALE MOUTH, STILL FULL BUT SLIGHTLY TOUGHER AND MORE MODERN

THE PUFFY LIPS OF A SULTRY CHARACTER. NOTE THAT EVERYTHING IS PUFFED OUT AND MORE CURVY; THE CORNERS ARE LOST IN THE UPPER AND LOWER LIPS

CARTOONING THE FACE

BUT SERIOUSLY -- WHO WANTS TO DRAW A NORMAL FACE? NOW THAT YOU'VE SEEN HOW INDIVIDUAL DETAILS IN A FACE CAN CREATE A DISTINCT CHARACTER AND PERSONALITY, TAKE A LOOK AT HOW THE OVERALL STRUCTURE OF A FACE CAN BE EXAGGERATED, ADJUSTED, AND CARTOONED!

NORMAL PARTS AND PROPORTIONS

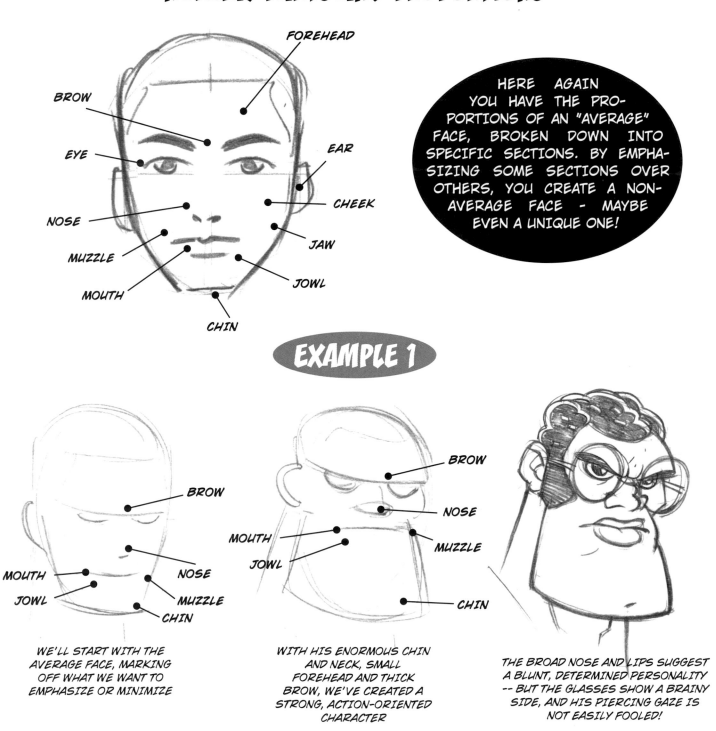

FOREHEAD
BROW
EYE
EAR
NOSE
CHEEK
MUZZLE
JAW
MOUTH
JOWL
CHIN

HERE AGAIN YOU HAVE THE PRO-PORTIONS OF AN "AVERAGE" FACE, BROKEN DOWN INTO SPECIFIC SECTIONS. BY EMPHA-SIZING SOME SECTIONS OVER OTHERS, YOU CREATE A NON-AVERAGE FACE - MAYBE EVEN A UNIQUE ONE!

EXAMPLE 1

BROW
MOUTH
JOWL
NOSE
MUZZLE
CHIN

WE'LL START WITH THE AVERAGE FACE, MARKING OFF WHAT WE WANT TO EMPHASIZE OR MINIMIZE

BROW
NOSE
MOUTH
MUZZLE
JOWL
CHIN

WITH HIS ENORMOUS CHIN AND NECK, SMALL FOREHEAD AND THICK BROW, WE'VE CREATED A STRONG, ACTION-ORIENTED CHARACTER

THE BROAD NOSE AND LIPS SUGGEST A BLUNT, DETERMINED PERSONALITY -- BUT THE GLASSES SHOW A BRAINY SIDE, AND HIS PIERCING GAZE IS NOT EASILY FOOLED!

EXAMPLE 2

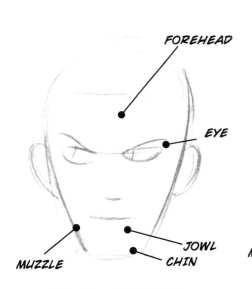

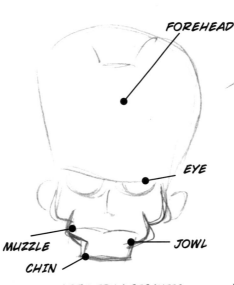

ANOTHER AVERAGE FACE, MARKING OFF WHAT WE WANT TO EMPHASIZE OR MINIMIZE

LET'S TRY A GIGANTIC FOREHEAD, LARGE EYES, SHARP CHEEKS AND FLABBY JOWLS, WITH A TINY CHIN

THE WIDE, WRINKLED FOREHEAD AND SHIFTY EYES BELONG TO A SCHEMER. THE LARGE MOUTH IS WOBBLY, AND WITH THE FLABBY MUZZLE AND JOWLS SUGGEST A NERVOUS, DISHONEST PERSONALITY. FINALLY, THE WEAK CHIN SHOWS LACK OF DETERMINATION

EXAMPLE 3

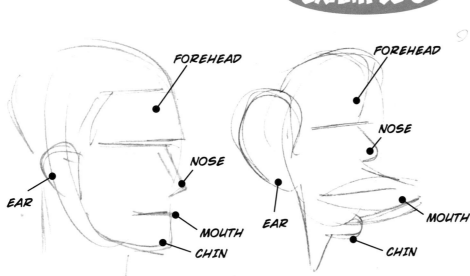

ONE LAST AVERAGE FACE, MARKING OFF WHAT WE WANT TO EMPHASIZE OR MINIMIZE

THIS WILL BE A SMOOTH-TALKING "BIG MOUTH," SO LET'S START WITH A BIG MOUTH, AND BIG EARS TO BALANCE IT OUT. A SMALL FOREHEAD, NOSE, AND RECEDING CHIN WILL MAKE THE MOUTH LOOK EVEN LARGER

PUSHING THE FOREHEAD AND HAIR FORWARD ON TOP BALANCES THE FORWARD -- JUTTING MOUTH BELOW. BUT WHILE THIS GUY HAS THE WRINKLED BROW AND WEAK CHIN OF THE SCHEMER ABOVE, HIS BROKEN NOSE, PUPPY EYES AND BENIGN SMILE MAKE HIM UNIQUE

ON THE NEXT FEW PAGES ARE STEP-BY-STEP EXAMPLES OF FOUR CLASSIC FACE "TYPES" AS WELL AS VARIATIONS THAT SHOW DIFFERENT WAYS TO CUSTOMIZE THOSE BASIC FACES...

HEROIC

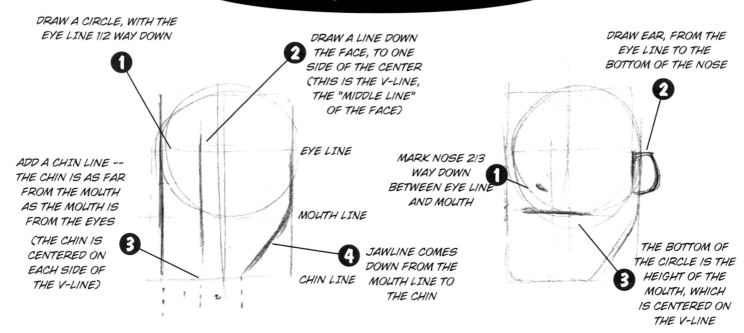

1 DRAW A CIRCLE, WITH THE EYE LINE 1/2 WAY DOWN

2 DRAW A LINE DOWN THE FACE, TO ONE SIDE OF THE CENTER (THIS IS THE V-LINE, THE "MIDDLE LINE" OF THE FACE)

EYE LINE

MOUTH LINE

3 ADD A CHIN LINE -- THE CHIN IS AS FAR FROM THE MOUTH AS THE MOUTH IS FROM THE EYES

(THE CHIN IS CENTERED ON EACH SIDE OF THE V-LINE)

CHIN LINE

4 JAWLINE COMES DOWN FROM THE MOUTH LINE TO THE CHIN

STEP 1

2 DRAW EAR, FROM THE EYE LINE TO THE BOTTOM OF THE NOSE

1 MARK NOSE 2/3 WAY DOWN BETWEEN EYE LINE AND MOUTH

3 THE BOTTOM OF THE CIRCLE IS THE HEIGHT OF THE MOUTH, WHICH IS CENTERED ON THE V-LINE

STEP 2

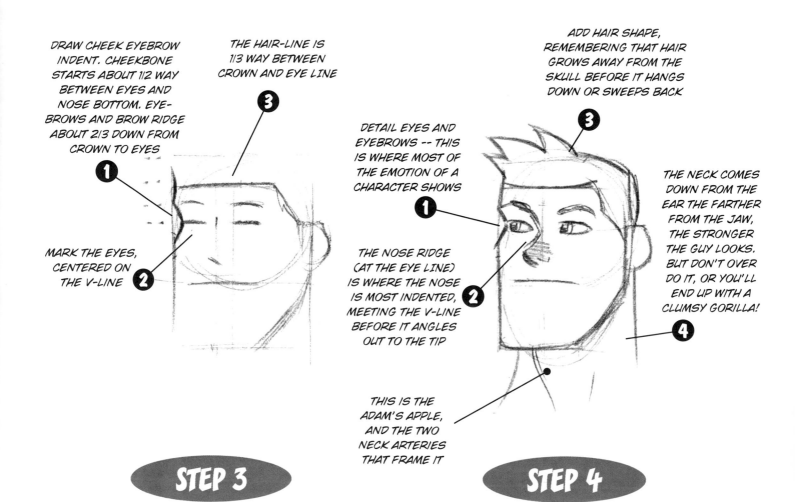

1 DRAW CHEEK EYEBROW INDENT. CHEEKBONE STARTS ABOUT 1/2 WAY BETWEEN EYES AND NOSE BOTTOM. EYE-BROWS AND BROW RIDGE ABOUT 2/3 DOWN FROM CROWN TO EYES

3 THE HAIR-LINE IS 1/3 WAY BETWEEN CROWN AND EYE LINE

2 MARK THE EYES, CENTERED ON THE V-LINE

STEP 3

3 ADD HAIR SHAPE, REMEMBERING THAT HAIR GROWS AWAY FROM THE SKULL BEFORE IT HANGS DOWN OR SWEEPS BACK

1 DETAIL EYES AND EYEBROWS -- THIS IS WHERE MOST OF THE EMOTION OF A CHARACTER SHOWS

2 THE NOSE RIDGE (AT THE EYE LINE) IS WHERE THE NOSE IS MOST INDENTED, MEETING THE V-LINE BEFORE IT ANGLES OUT TO THE TIP

4 THE NECK COMES DOWN FROM THE EAR THE FARTHER FROM THE JAW, THE STRONGER THE GUY LOOKS. BUT DON'T OVER DO IT, OR YOU'LL END UP WITH A CLUMSY GORILLA!

THIS IS THE ADAM'S APPLE, AND THE TWO NECK ARTERIES THAT FRAME IT

STEP 4

VARIATIONS

BY SOFTENING THE LINES OF THE FACE, AND GIVING YOUR CHARACTER MORE FEMININE LIPS AND EYES, YOU CAN CREATE THE "ROMEO" LOOK OF A MOVIE STAR.

ON THE OTHER HAND, BY KEEPING THE FACE LINES AND EDGE OF THE FACE STRAIGHT, YOU CREATE A MUCH MORE IMPOSING FIGURE. WITH HIS EXCESSIVELY HARSH EYEBROWS, DETERMINED, MASSIVE CHIN AND JAGGED NOSE, YOU CREATE A DANGEROUS, EVIL SPY.

HERE'S A CLASSIC THUG -- WITH A SMALL FOREHEAD AND LOW BROW, AND A STUMPY, BROKEN NOSE. HIS THICK NECK AND HUGE CHIN MAKE HIM LOOK STRONGER THAN THE HERO OPPOSITE, BUT HE ALSO LOOKS MORE CLUMSY AND DULL-WITTED.

THIS MAN'S AGE IS REVEALED BY HIS WRINKLES, RECEDING HAIR, AND HIS SAGGING JOWELS. BUT HIS STRONG CHIN AND BLUNT NOSE SUGGEST STRENGTH, WHILE THE GENTLE CURVES OF HIS FACE ARE A REMINDER OF A SMOOTH PERSONALITY. PERHAPS HE IS AN OLDER VERSION OF ROMEO ABOVE.

CUTE

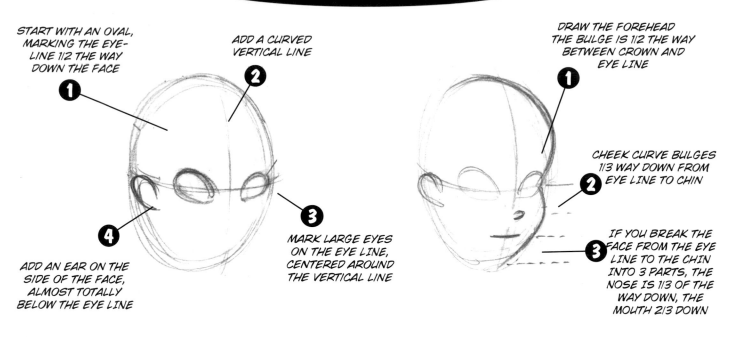

START WITH AN OVAL, MARKING THE EYE-LINE 1/2 THE WAY DOWN THE FACE ①

ADD A CURVED VERTICAL LINE ②

MARK LARGE EYES ON THE EYE LINE, CENTERED AROUND THE VERTICAL LINE ③

ADD AN EAR ON THE SIDE OF THE FACE, ALMOST TOTALLY BELOW THE EYE LINE ④

DRAW THE FOREHEAD THE BULGE IS 1/2 THE WAY BETWEEN CROWN AND EYE LINE ①

CHEEK CURVE BULGES 1/3 WAY DOWN FROM EYE LINE TO CHIN ②

IF YOU BREAK THE FACE FROM THE EYE LINE TO THE CHIN INTO 3 PARTS, THE NOSE IS 1/3 OF THE WAY DOWN, THE MOUTH 2/3 DOWN ③

STEP 1 **STEP 2**

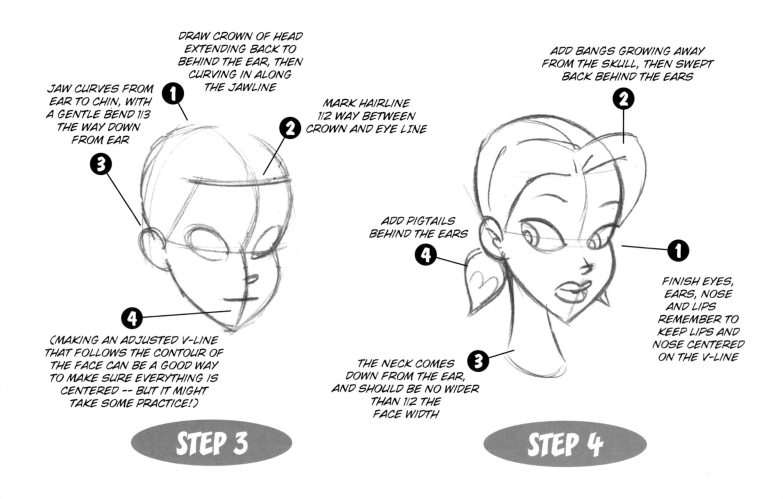

JAW CURVES FROM EAR TO CHIN, WITH A GENTLE BEND 1/3 THE WAY DOWN FROM EAR ③

DRAW CROWN OF HEAD EXTENDING BACK TO BEHIND THE EAR, THEN CURVING IN ALONG THE JAWLINE ①

MARK HAIRLINE 1/2 WAY BETWEEN CROWN AND EYE LINE ②

(MAKING AN ADJUSTED V-LINE THAT FOLLOWS THE CONTOUR OF THE FACE CAN BE A GOOD WAY TO MAKE SURE EVERYTHING IS CENTERED -- BUT IT MIGHT TAKE SOME PRACTICE!) ④

ADD BANGS GROWING AWAY FROM THE SKULL, THEN SWEPT BACK BEHIND THE EARS ②

ADD PIGTAILS BEHIND THE EARS ④

FINISH EYES, EARS, NOSE AND LIPS REMEMBER TO KEEP LIPS AND NOSE CENTERED ON THE V-LINE ①

THE NECK COMES DOWN FROM THE EAR, AND SHOULD BE NO WIDER THAN 1/2 THE FACE WIDTH ③

STEP 3 **STEP 4**

VARIATIONS

THE CUTE TYPE SUGGESTS YOUTH AND INNOCENCE BECAUSE IT FOLLOWS THE BASIC PROPORTIONS OF A CHILD. THE LITTLE BOY (LEFT) IS JUST A WIDER VERSION OF THE CUTE GIRL, WITH BIGGER CHEEKS AND A SMALLER NOSE. (SMALLER FOREHEAD, CHEEKS AND EYES MAKE A CHARACTER LOOK OLDER. SO DO BIGGER CHINS AND NOSES)

THIS TOMBOY HAS THE BASIC CUTE PROPORTIONS, BUT HER LONGER FACE WITH ITS STRONG NOSE, EYEBROWS AND CHIN SUGGEST A TOUGH SIDE. THIS IS OFFSET BY HER FEMININE LIPS AND EYELASHES

A WIDE, CUTE FACE CAN STILL LOOK SOPHISTICATED. ONE SUGGESTION IS TO DE-EMPHASIZE THE CHEEK AND FOREHEAD BULGES. A LONG, SLENDER NECK IS ALSO A GOOD WAY TO SHOW GRACE, WHILE HALF-CLOSED EYES IMPLY THE BORED CHARM OF AN ELEGANT LADY

EVEN A YOUNG HERO CAN HAVE "CUTE" PROPORTIONS, WHICH EMPHASIZE THE YOUTH AND INEXPERIENCE OF A CHARACTER. THIS APPROACH WORKS ESPECIALLY WELL WITH TEENS OR OTHER "ROOKIE" HEROES WHO RELY ON BRAINS OR LUCK OVER BRAWN

PUDGY CHEEKS AREN'T JUST FOR BABIES. SEPARATING THEM FROM THE CHIN MAKES THIS LADY LOOK OLDER (ALONG WITH THE 1950S HAIRDO, GLASSES, AND ASCOT). BUT THE BASICALLY CHILDLIKE PROPORTIONS OF HER FACE SHOW THIS LADY TO BE PERKY, WHATEVER HER AGE

GAUNT

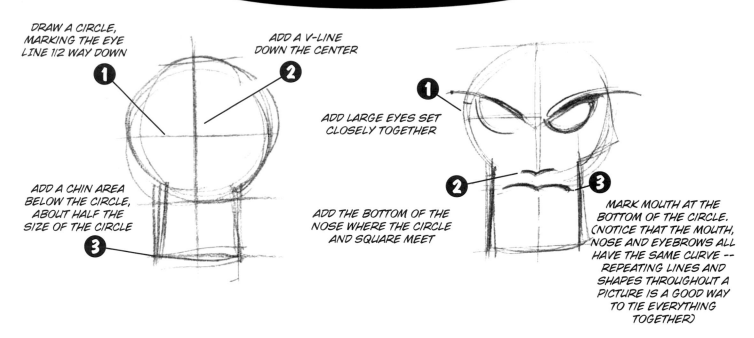

DRAW A CIRCLE, MARKING THE EYE LINE 1/2 WAY DOWN

1

ADD A V-LINE DOWN THE CENTER

2

ADD A CHIN AREA BELOW THE CIRCLE, ABOUT HALF THE SIZE OF THE CIRCLE

3

ADD LARGE EYES SET CLOSELY TOGETHER

1

ADD THE BOTTOM OF THE NOSE WHERE THE CIRCLE AND SQUARE MEET

2 **3**

MARK MOUTH AT THE BOTTOM OF THE CIRCLE. (NOTICE THAT THE MOUTH, NOSE AND EYEBROWS ALL HAVE THE SAME CURVE -- REPEATING LINES AND SHAPES THROUGHOUT A PICTURE IS A GOOD WAY TO TIE EVERYTHING TOGETHER)

STEP 1

STEP 2

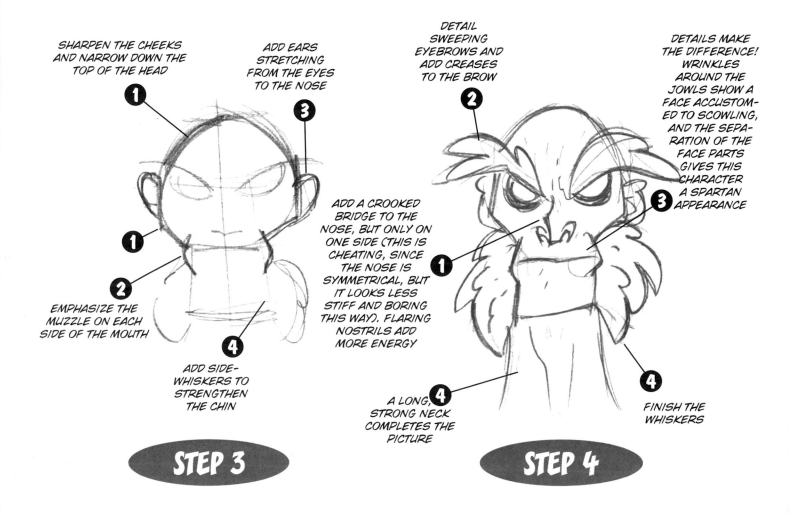

SHARPEN THE CHEEKS AND NARROW DOWN THE TOP OF THE HEAD

1

ADD EARS STRETCHING FROM THE EYES TO THE NOSE

3

1

EMPHASIZE THE MUZZLE ON EACH SIDE OF THE MOUTH

2

ADD SIDE-WHISKERS TO STRENGTHEN THE CHIN

4

DETAIL SWEEPING EYEBROWS AND ADD CREASES TO THE BROW

2

ADD A CROOKED BRIDGE TO THE NOSE, BUT ONLY ON ONE SIDE (THIS IS CHEATING, SINCE THE NOSE IS SYMMETRICAL, BUT IT LOOKS LESS STIFF AND BORING THIS WAY). FLARING NOSTRILS ADD MORE ENERGY

1

A LONG, STRONG NECK COMPLETES THE PICTURE

4

DETAILS MAKE THE DIFFERENCE! WRINKLES AROUND THE JOWLS SHOW A FACE ACCUSTOMED TO SCOWLING, AND THE SEPARATION OF THE FACE PARTS GIVES THIS CHARACTER A SPARTAN APPEARANCE

3

FINISH THE WHISKERS

4

STEP 3

STEP 4

VARIATIONS

(LEFT) THIS BRUISER IS LEAN, BUT MEAN. HIS THICK NECK AND BROKEN NOSE SUGGEST A FIGHTER RATHER THAN A SCHEMER. MASSIVE EYE-BROWS AND EARS HELP EMPHASIZE HIS PAR-TICULAR PERSONALITY

DE-EMPHASIZING THE NECK AND CHIN CREATES A LESS AGGRESSIVE CHARACTER. THIS ARTSY OLD BAT IS GAUNT, BUT HER PROPORTIONS ARE FAIRLY CLOSE TO NORMAL, SO SHE APPEARS OLD WITHOUT BEING GROTESQUE OR SINISTER

GAUNT FACES ARE USUALLY ASSOCIATED WITH SINISTER OR SICKLY CHARACTERS BECAUSE THEY RESEMBLE A SKULL -- THE ULTIMATE SYMBOL OF DEATH

CONTRASTING THE GAUNTNESS OF THIS AFRICAN KING'S FACE WITH A BROAD NOSE AND LIPS SUGGESTS INNER STRENGTH AND PERSEVERANCE, WITHOUT A TRACE OF FRAILTY OR FLAB

A WIDE, FAIRLY SOFT FACE CAN STILL BE GAUNT. HERE THE SAGGING JOWLS AND CHEEKS ARE SEPARATED AND LINED WITH AGE, AND ADD A CERTAIN STRENGTH TO THE RELATIVELY SMALL CHIN OF THIS OLD, RETIRED VAMPIRE

HEAVY

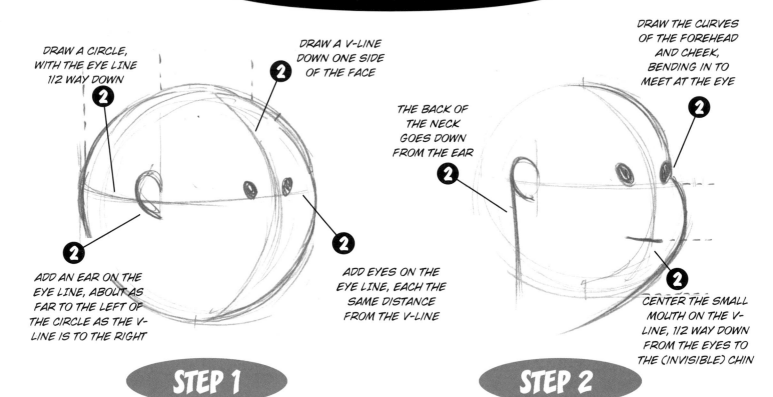

DRAW A CIRCLE, WITH THE EYE LINE 1/2 WAY DOWN ❷

DRAW A V-LINE DOWN ONE SIDE OF THE FACE ❷

ADD AN EAR ON THE EYE LINE, ABOUT AS FAR TO THE LEFT OF THE CIRCLE AS THE V-LINE IS TO THE RIGHT ❷

ADD EYES ON THE EYE LINE, EACH THE SAME DISTANCE FROM THE V-LINE ❷

STEP 1

DRAW THE CURVES OF THE FOREHEAD AND CHEEK, BENDING IN TO MEET AT THE EYE ❷

THE BACK OF THE NECK GOES DOWN FROM THE EAR ❷

CENTER THE SMALL MOUTH ON THE V-LINE, 1/2 WAY DOWN FROM THE EYES TO THE (INVISIBLE) CHIN ❷

STEP 2

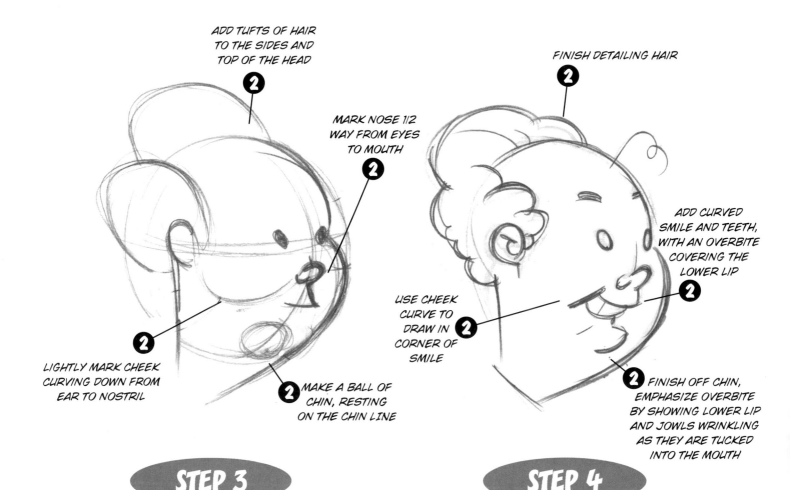

ADD TUFTS OF HAIR TO THE SIDES AND TOP OF THE HEAD ❷

MARK NOSE 1/2 WAY FROM EYES TO MOUTH ❷

LIGHTLY MARK CHEEK CURVING DOWN FROM EAR TO NOSTRIL ❷

MAKE A BALL OF CHIN, RESTING ON THE CHIN LINE ❷

STEP 3

FINISH DETAILING HAIR ❷

ADD CURVED SMILE AND TEETH, WITH AN OVERBITE COVERING THE LOWER LIP ❷

USE CHEEK CURVE TO DRAW IN CORNER OF SMILE ❷

FINISH OFF CHIN, EMPHASIZE OVERBITE BY SHOWING LOWER LIP AND JOWLS WRINKLING AS THEY ARE TUCKED INTO THE MOUTH ❷

STEP 4

VARIATIONS

ON THIS OLDER FACE THE FLAB IS SAGGING, ALMOST LEVEL WITH THE CHIN. THE BROKEN NOSE, STRONG BROW AND FLAB-FREE NECK SUGGEST A BEEFY **COWBOY** WHO'S GONE TO SEED

WHILE THIS GIRL HAS A HEAVY FACE, HER DISTINCT CHIN, CHEEKS AND JAW SUGGEST A NATURALLY WIDE FACE. THE "SECOND CHIN" IS CLEARLY SEPARATE FROM THE NECK, AND COMBINES WITH THE CHIN TO SUGGEST A STUBBORN, STRONG PERSONALITY

HIS CHEEKS AND SECOND CHIN ARE HEAVIER THAN IN THE GIRL ABOVE, BUT THIS GUY'S STRONG CHIN AND NOSE HELP TO KEEP THIS **JOKESTER'S** FACE FROM GETTING LOST IN THE FLAB

THIS **FREAKISH VILLAIN** HAS SHARP FEATURES THAT ARE ALMOST COMPLETELY DROWNED OUT BY HIS EXTRA FLESH. THE CHEEKS, CHIN AND NECK ARE A SINGLE CURVE, AND HIS FEATURES LOOK LIKE THEY ARE HALF-SUNK INTO HIS FACE. SICKLY EYES AND SHARP LIPS COMPLETE HIS BIZARRELY SINISTER APPEARANCE

ANIMAL MAGNETISM

WE LIKE TO THINK THAT DIFFERENT ANIMALS HAVE SPECIFIC PERSONALITIES -- A MOUSE IS MEEK, A LION IS NOBLE, A DOG IS LOYAL, AND SO ON. MAKING A HUMAN PHYSICALLY RESEMBLE A PARTICULAR ANIMAL IS A GOOD WAY TO SUBTLY SUGGEST THAT THE CHARACTER SHARES THAT ANIMAL'S PERSONALITY. CONSIDER THE TWO EXAMPLES BELOW...

EXAMPLE 1

WHAT COULD BE MORE STUPID AND BRUTISH THAN A THUG? HOW ABOUT A THUG WHO LOOKS LIKE A GORILLA!

EXAMPLE 2

NOTHING SAYS SNEAKY LIKE A RAT. SO NO ONE LOOKS SNEAKIER THAN A GUY WITH A RAT-LIKE FACE...

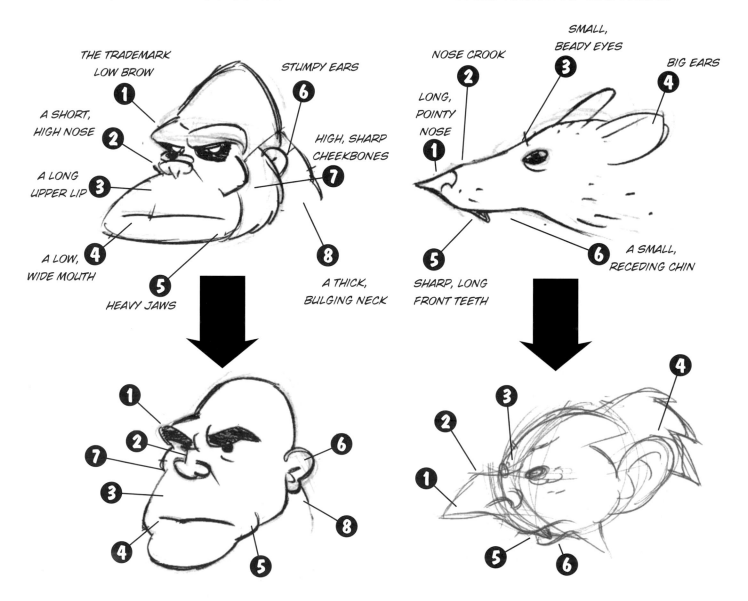

SNEAKY RAT

START WITH A CIRCLE, BISECTED WITH AN EYE LINE AND A V-LINE DIVIDING THE FACE INTO 2 SIDES. **1**

ADD SMALL EYES, CENTERED ON EACH SIDE OF THE V-LINE **2**

ADD A LONG, POINTY NOSE COMING FROM THE V-LINE, WITH THE TOP AT THE EYE LINE AND THE BOTTOM HALFWAY FROM THE EYE LINE TO THE CHIN **1**

PLACE A GIANT RAT EAR ON THE SIDE OF THE HEAD **2**

MARK A TWISTED MOUTH 2 3 DOWN FROM THE NOSE LINE TO THE CHIN **3**

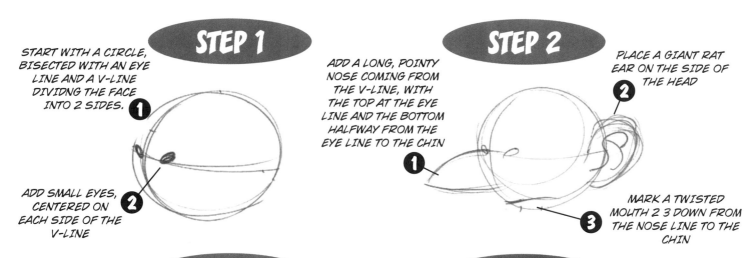

TWO GIANT TUFTS OF HAIR BURST OUT FROM BEHIND THE EARS (YOU CAN'T SEE THE OTHER EAR, BUT YOU CAN GUESS WHERE IT WOULD BE, AND PLACE A TUFT BEHIND IT) **1**

ADD RAT TEETH AND A TINY, SHARP CHIN **2**

A SCRAWNY NECK STRETCHES DOWN FROM HIS CHIN AND EAR **3**

SHARPEN THE NOSE AND ADD LARGE NOSTRILS, THE KIND A RAT WOULD SNIFF WITH **1**

FLATTEN THE FOREHEAD AND ADD EYEBROWS **2**

DETAIL THE TUFTS OF HAIR **3**

DON'T FORGET A SHARP LITTLE JAW! **4**

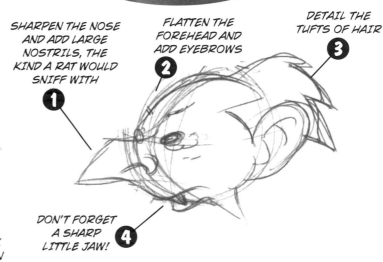

OF COURSE, SOMETIMES YOU WANT TO AVOID CERTAIN ANIMAL ASSOCIATIONS. THE TWO LADIES ON THE RIGHT LOOK BASICALLY THE SAME. BUT EXAMPLE 2 LOOKS A LITTLE LESS INTELLIGENT AND GRACEFUL THAN EXAMPLE 1. THE REASON? HER UPPER LIP IS TOO LONG, REMINDING US OF THOSE BEAUTY-CHALLENGED GORILLAS. MANY TIMES THESE SORTS OF PROBLEMS ARE TOO SUBTLE TO NOTICE SOMETHING WILL JUST LOOK "OFF." ONLY A LOT OF PRACTICE AND ATTENTION TO PROPORTIONS WILL FIX IT.

EXAMPLE 1

EXAMPLE 2

DRAWING EMOTIONS

ONCE AGAIN, WE HAVE AN AVERAGE FACE BROKEN INTO SECTIONS. BUT HERE THE FOCUS IS ON HOW THE PARTS OF THE FACE MOVE AND WRINKLE TO REFLECT VARIOUS EMOTIONS.

DIVIDING WRINKLES IN AN UNEMOTIONAL FACE

A "BLANK" FACE

A FACE IS LIKE THE SURFACE OF THE EARTH -- IT'S MADE UP OF PARTS THAT MEET AT WRINKLES, JUST LIKE THE PARTS OF THE EARTH MEET AT FAULTS. WHEN MUSCLES UNDER THE SKIN MOVE IN ANGER, FEAR, JOY, ETC., THE SURFACE PARTS OF OUR FACE MOVE, TOO. THEN THE WRINKLES THAT SEPARATE THEM DEEPEN, MOVE OR CREASE IN RESPONSE. THE MORE WE MAKE CERTAIN EXPRESSIONS, THE MORE THE WRINKLES THAT SHOW THOSE EXPRESSIONS STAY ETCHED IN OUR FACE. YOU DON'T WANT TO SHOW EVERY WRINKLE ALL THE TIME, OR YOUR CHARACTERS WILL ALL LOOK OLD. BUT THE RIGHT COMBINATION OF WRINKLES CAN EXPRESS ANY EMOTION.

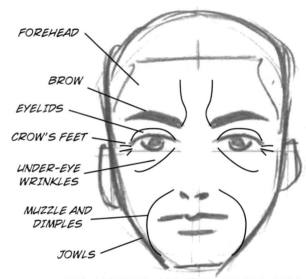

FOREHEAD
BROW
EYELIDS
CROW'S FEET
UNDER-EYE WRINKLES
MUZZLE AND DIMPLES
JOWLS

THE VARIOUS WRINKLES ON THE FACE (DON'T USE THEM ALL AT ONCE!)

SMILING

WHEN YOU SMILE, THE CORNERS OF YOUR MOUTH GO UP AND OUT, PUSHING YOUR CHEEKS UP TO YOUR EYES AND CREATING WRINKLES AT THE CORNERS OF YOUR MOUTH AND BOTTOM OF YOUR EYES. THE BROWS ALSO RISE UP AND OUT, CREATING WRINKLES ON THE OUTER EDGES OF THE FOREHEAD.

SHOUTING

WHEN YELLING, THE LIPS DRAW BACK FROM THE TEETH AND THE CHIN JUTS OUT, AS MAJOR CREASES SHOW FROM THE CHIN TO THE MUZZLE. THIS ALSO MAKES THE CHEEKS SCRUNCH UP, CAUSING WRINKLES AROUND THE EYES. FINALLY, AN ANGRY, LOWERED BROW WRINKLES IN THE CENTER, AS DOES THE BRIDGE OF THE NOSE AND THE NEARBY PARTS OF THE EYES.

SCOWLING

A QUIET BUT INTENSE COMPANION TO THE YELL, THE SCOWL FOCUSES MORE ON THE BROW THAN THE MOUTH, WITH HEAVY CREASES AND WRINKLES SLANTING DOWN TO THE CENTER OF THE BROW. THESE ARE REINFORCED BY THE WRINKLES AROUND THE EYES AND BRIDGE OF THE NOSE THAT ALSO SLANT DOWN AND IN. THE BOTTOM OF THE NOSE SCREWS UP, EXAGGERATING THE NOSTRILS AND CAUSING THE UPPER LIP TO CURL INTO A SLIGHT SNEER, WHICH CAUSES ITS OWN CREASE BY THE NOSTRIL.

FRIGHTENED

LIKE A SMILING FACE, A FRIGHTENED FACE MOVES OUTWARD, BUT IN EVERY DIRECTION. THE BROW PUSHES THE ENTIRE FOREHEAD UP AND OUT, SO THAT THE SLANT OF THE HEAD ITSELF IS EXAGGERATED. THE EYES ARE HUGE -- ALERT TO DANGER -- WITH WRINKLES UNDERNEATH. FINALLY, THE MOUTH PEELS BACK FROM THE TEETH AND DROOPS AT THE EDGES, WRINKLING THE CHIN AND MAKING IT SMALLER (AND WEAKER).

AGE

THE PROPORTIONS AND SHAPES OF THE FACE CHANGE AS PEOPLE GET OLDER. BEING ABLE TO DRAW CHARACTERS THAT LOOK THEIR AGE IS ONE OF THE MOST DIFFICULT -- AND OVERLOOKED -- SKILLS OF CARTOONING!

YOUNGER FACES

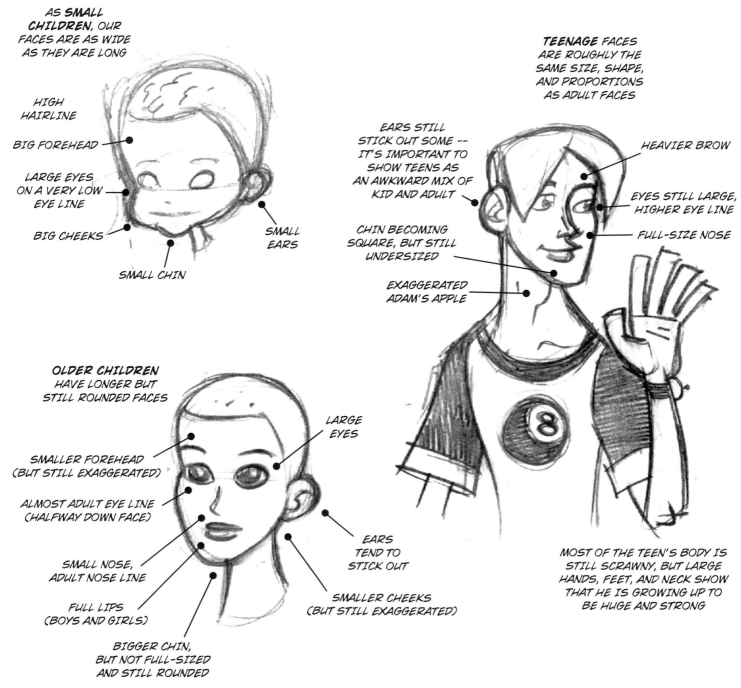

AS **SMALL CHILDREN**, OUR FACES ARE AS WIDE AS THEY ARE LONG

HIGH HAIRLINE

BIG FOREHEAD

LARGE EYES ON A VERY LOW EYE LINE

BIG CHEEKS

SMALL CHIN

SMALL EARS

TEENAGE FACES ARE ROUGHLY THE SAME SIZE, SHAPE, AND PROPORTIONS AS ADULT FACES

EARS STILL STICK OUT SOME -- IT'S IMPORTANT TO SHOW TEENS AS AN AWKWARD MIX OF KID AND ADULT

CHIN BECOMING SQUARE, BUT STILL UNDERSIZED

EXAGGERATED ADAM'S APPLE

HEAVIER BROW

EYES STILL LARGE, HIGHER EYE LINE

FULL-SIZE NOSE

OLDER CHILDREN HAVE LONGER BUT STILL ROUNDED FACES

SMALLER FOREHEAD (BUT STILL EXAGGERATED)

ALMOST ADULT EYE LINE (HALFWAY DOWN FACE)

SMALL NOSE, ADULT NOSE LINE

FULL LIPS (BOYS AND GIRLS)

BIGGER CHIN, BUT NOT FULL-SIZED AND STILL ROUNDED

LARGE EYES

EARS TEND TO STICK OUT

SMALLER CHEEKS (BUT STILL EXAGGERATED)

MOST OF THE TEEN'S BODY IS STILL SCRAWNY, BUT LARGE HANDS, FEET, AND NECK SHOW THAT HE IS GROWING UP TO BE HUGE AND STRONG

ADULT FACES

HEROIC **ADULTS** GENERALLY HAVE EXAGGERATED CHINS AND BROWS, AND SMALLER FOREHEADS

MIDDLE-AGED ADULTS HAVE HEAVIER FEATURES, AND THE PARTS OF THE FACE BECOME MORE DISTINCT FROM ONE ANOTHER

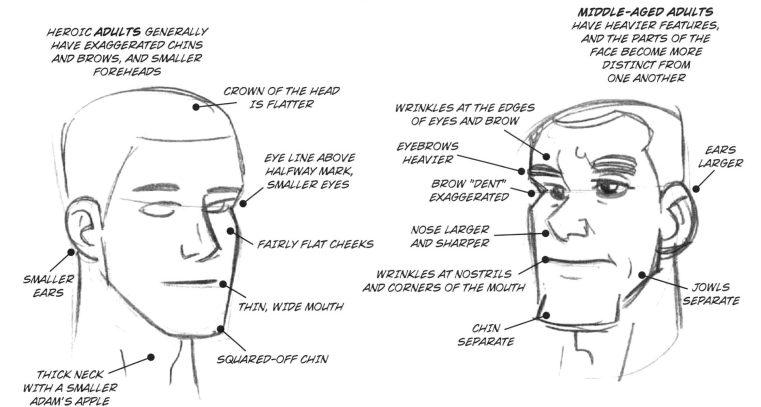

CROWN OF THE HEAD IS FLATTER

EYE LINE ABOVE HALFWAY MARK, SMALLER EYES

FAIRLY FLAT CHEEKS

SMALLER EARS

THIN, WIDE MOUTH

THICK NECK WITH A SMALLER ADAM'S APPLE

SQUARED-OFF CHIN

WRINKLES AT THE EDGES OF EYES AND BROW

EYEBROWS HEAVIER

BROW "DENT" EXAGGERATED

NOSE LARGER AND SHARPER

WRINKLES AT NOSTRILS AND CORNERS OF THE MOUTH

CHIN SEPARATE

EARS LARGER

JOWLS SEPARATE

OLDER FACES

OLD GEEZERS HAVE EVEN MORE DISTINCTIONS BETWEEN FACE PARTS

REMEMBER THAT WRINKLES ARE A RECORD OF A PERSON'S EMOTIONS AND PERSONALITY. A PERSON WHO SMILES HIS WHOLE LIFE WILL HAVE ONE SET OF WRINKLES, A PERSON WHO SCOWLS WILL HAVE AN ENTIRELY DIFFERENT SET!

SOFT OR ANGULAR LINES GO A LONG WAY TOWARDS DEFINING THE KIND OF GRANDPA YOU CREATE

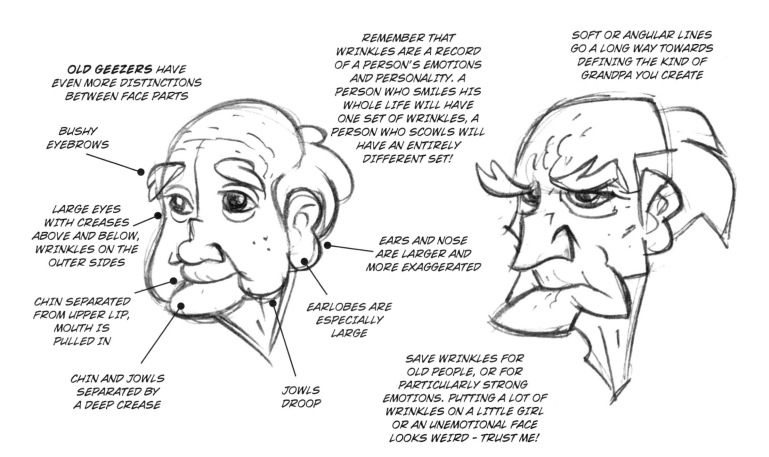

BUSHY EYEBROWS

LARGE EYES WITH CREASES ABOVE AND BELOW, WRINKLES ON THE OUTER SIDES

CHIN SEPARATED FROM UPPER LIP, MOUTH IS PULLED IN

CHIN AND JOWLS SEPARATED BY A DEEP CREASE

EARS AND NOSE ARE LARGER AND MORE EXAGGERATED

EARLOBES ARE ESPECIALLY LARGE

JOWLS DROOP

SAVE WRINKLES FOR OLD PEOPLE, OR FOR PARTICULARLY STRONG EMOTIONS. PUTTING A LOT OF WRINKLES ON A LITTLE GIRL OR AN UNEMOTIONAL FACE LOOKS WEIRD - TRUST ME!

THE BODY!

WE'VE ALL GOT 'EM, LET'S DRAW 'EM! THE BODY COMES IN ALL SHAPES AND SIZES, BUT IT'S ALWAYS MADE UP OF THE SAME PARTS MOVING IN THE SAME WAYS. IN THIS SECTION WE'LL LOOK AT THESE PARTS, HOW THEY FIT TOGETHER, AND WHAT THEY LOOK LIKE WHEN YOU MOVE THEM!

THE BASIC BODY

LIKE THE FACE, THE BODY SHOULD BE SEEN IN ITS "NORMAL" FORM BEFORE WE ALTER IT TO CREATE DIFFERENT KINDS OF CHARACTERS. BELOW ARE THE STANDARD SHAPES AND PROPORTIONS OF THE BODY. ON THE NEXT PAGE ARE THE SHAPES AND PROPORTIONS OF A STANDARD HEROIC CARTOON BODY.

FORMS AND PROPORTIONS

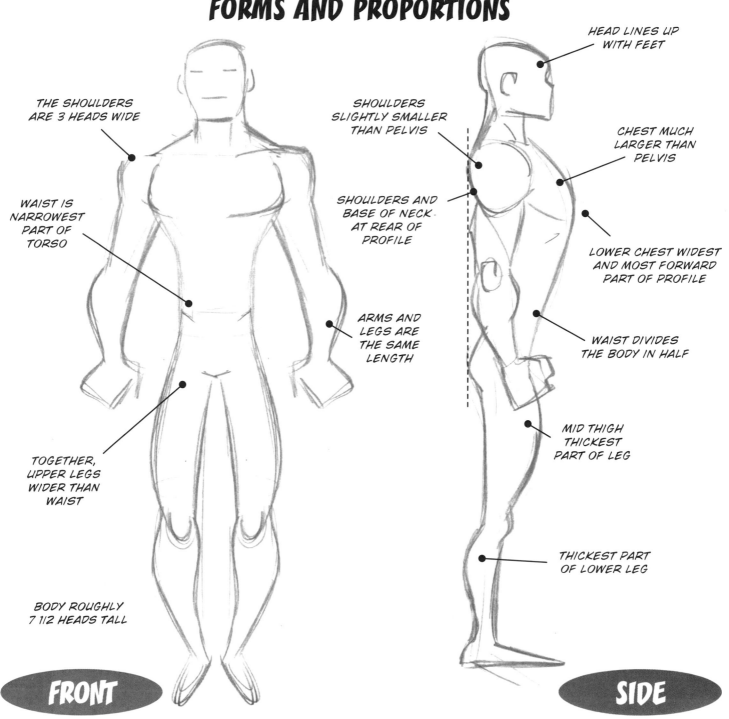

THE SHOULDERS ARE 3 HEADS WIDE

WAIST IS NARROWEST PART OF TORSO

TOGETHER, UPPER LEGS WIDER THAN WAIST

BODY ROUGHLY 7 1/2 HEADS TALL

ARMS AND LEGS ARE THE SAME LENGTH

HEAD LINES UP WITH FEET

SHOULDERS SLIGHTLY SMALLER THAN PELVIS

SHOULDERS AND BASE OF NECK AT REAR OF PROFILE

CHEST MUCH LARGER THAN PELVIS

LOWER CHEST WIDEST AND MOST FORWARD PART OF PROFILE

WAIST DIVIDES THE BODY IN HALF

MID THIGH THICKEST PART OF LEG

THICKEST PART OF LOWER LEG

FRONT

SIDE

THE MALE -- VARIATIONS

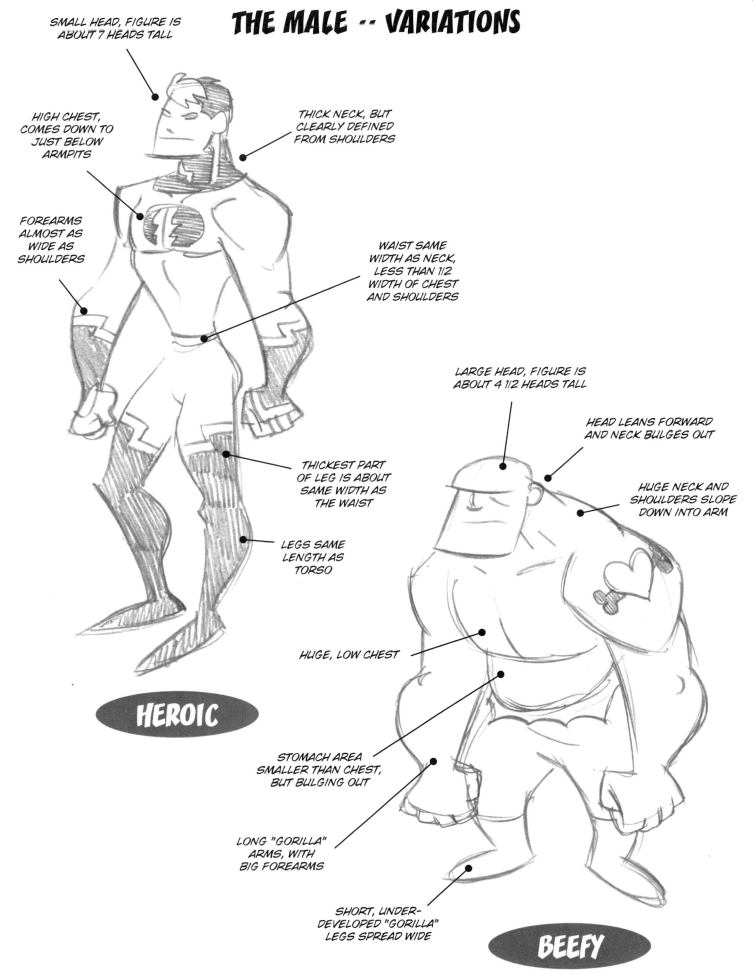

SMALL HEAD, FIGURE IS ABOUT 7 HEADS TALL

HIGH CHEST, COMES DOWN TO JUST BELOW ARMPITS

THICK NECK, BUT CLEARLY DEFINED FROM SHOULDERS

FOREARMS ALMOST AS WIDE AS SHOULDERS

WAIST SAME WIDTH AS NECK, LESS THAN 1/2 WIDTH OF CHEST AND SHOULDERS

THICKEST PART OF LEG IS ABOUT SAME WIDTH AS THE WAIST

LEGS SAME LENGTH AS TORSO

HEROIC

LARGE HEAD, FIGURE IS ABOUT 4 1/2 HEADS TALL

HEAD LEANS FORWARD AND NECK BULGES OUT

HUGE NECK AND SHOULDERS SLOPE DOWN INTO ARM

HUGE, LOW CHEST

STOMACH AREA SMALLER THAN CHEST, BUT BULGING OUT

LONG "GORILLA" ARMS, WITH BIG FOREARMS

SHORT, UNDER-DEVELOPED "GORILLA" LEGS SPREAD WIDE

BEEFY

THE MALE -- VARIATIONS

LARGE HEAD, FIGURE IS ABOUT 4 1/2 HEADS TALL

SHORT NECK SLOPES INTO NARROW, UN-DEFINED SHOULDERS

THICKEST PART OF ARM IS JUST ABOVE THE ELBOW

WAIST IS CURVED AND LOWEST IN FRONT, A LITTLE BELOW HALF-WAY DOWN THE BODY

SMALL HEAD, FIGURE IS ABOUT 6 1/2 HEADS TALL

WRISTS AND ANKLES REMAIN NARROW, HANDS AND FEET ARE SMALL

HEAVY

THIN NECK

THERE IS ALMOST NO CHANGE IN WIDTH OF TORSO FROM CHEST TO WAIST

NO HIPS!

THE MIDDLE PARTS OF THE ARMS AND LEGS ARE THIN, BUT THE JOINTS ARE LARGER

HANDS AND FEET ARE BIG, WITH LONG TOES AND FINGERS

SKINNY

THE FEMALE BODY

FORMS AND PROPORTIONS

FRONT

SIDE

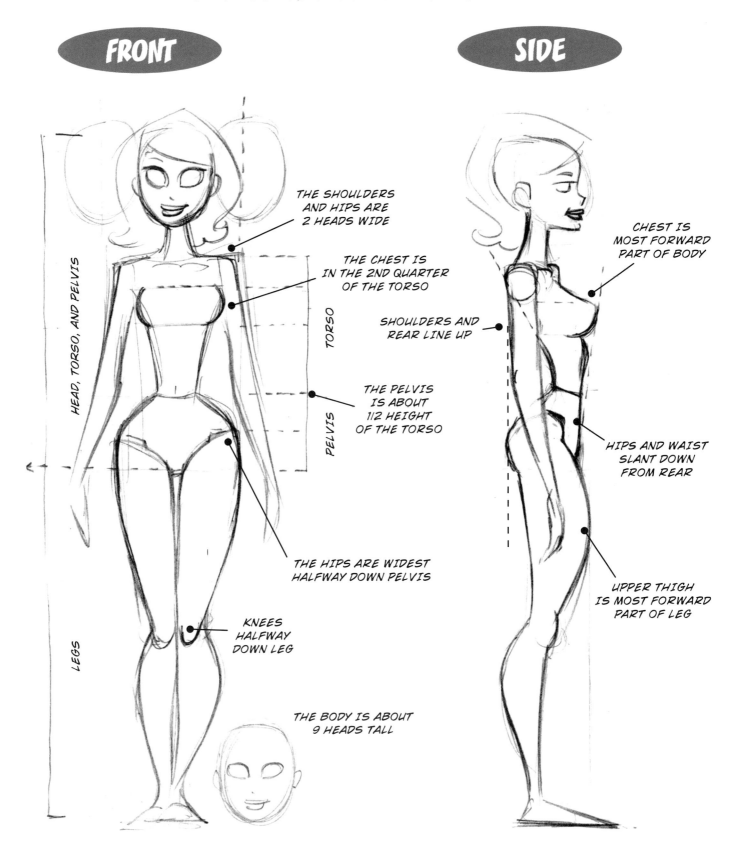

HEAD, TORSO, AND PELVIS

TORSO

PELVIS

LEGS

THE SHOULDERS AND HIPS ARE 2 HEADS WIDE

THE CHEST IS IN THE 2ND QUARTER OF THE TORSO

THE PELVIS IS ABOUT 1/2 HEIGHT OF THE TORSO

THE HIPS ARE WIDEST HALFWAY DOWN PELVIS

KNEES HALFWAY DOWN LEG

THE BODY IS ABOUT 9 HEADS TALL

CHEST IS MOST FORWARD PART OF BODY

SHOULDERS AND REAR LINE UP

HIPS AND WAIST SLANT DOWN FROM REAR

UPPER THIGH IS MOST FORWARD PART OF LEG

THE FEMALE -- VARIATIONS

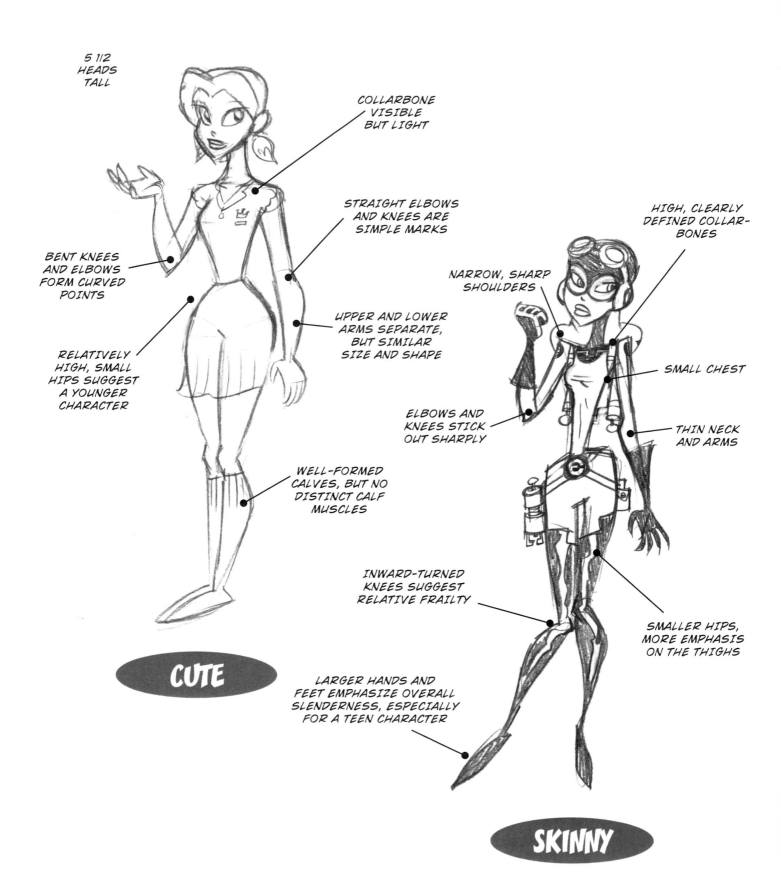

5 1/2 HEADS TALL

COLLARBONE VISIBLE BUT LIGHT

STRAIGHT ELBOWS AND KNEES ARE SIMPLE MARKS

BENT KNEES AND ELBOWS FORM CURVED POINTS

UPPER AND LOWER ARMS SEPARATE, BUT SIMILAR SIZE AND SHAPE

RELATIVELY HIGH, SMALL HIPS SUGGEST A YOUNGER CHARACTER

WELL-FORMED CALVES, BUT NO DISTINCT CALF MUSCLES

HIGH, CLEARLY DEFINED COLLAR-BONES

NARROW, SHARP SHOULDERS

SMALL CHEST

ELBOWS AND KNEES STICK OUT SHARPLY

THIN NECK AND ARMS

INWARD-TURNED KNEES SUGGEST RELATIVE FRAILTY

SMALLER HIPS, MORE EMPHASIS ON THE THIGHS

LARGER HANDS AND FEET EMPHASIZE OVERALL SLENDERNESS, ESPECIALLY FOR A TEEN CHARACTER

CUTE

SKINNY

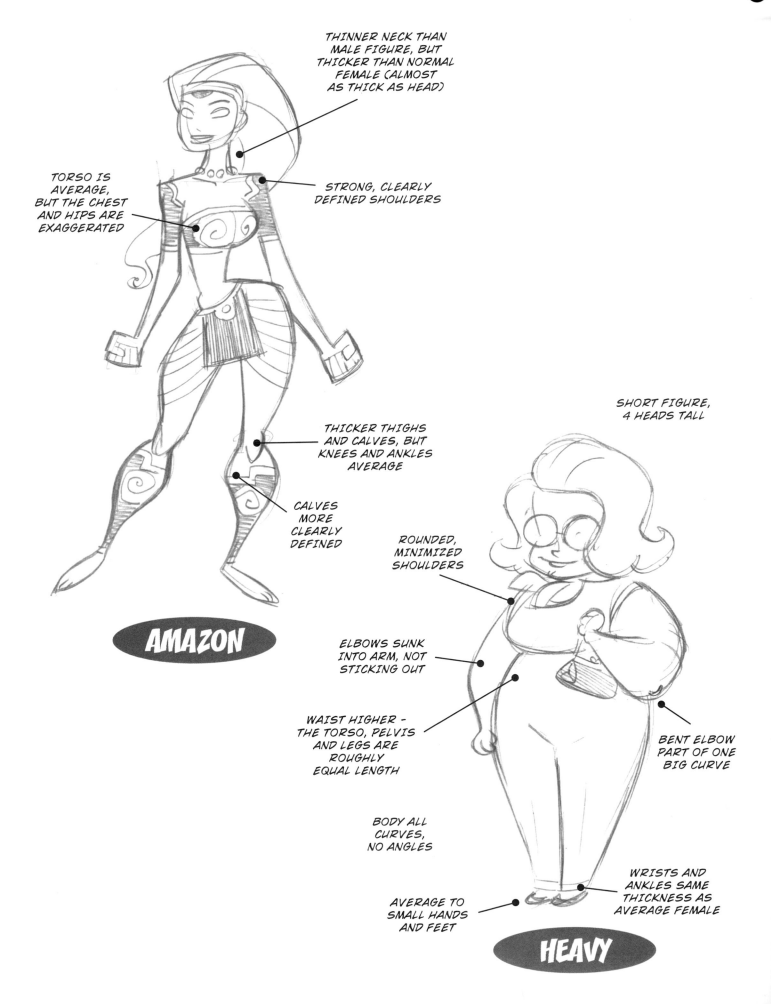

THINNER NECK THAN MALE FIGURE, BUT THICKER THAN NORMAL FEMALE (ALMOST AS THICK AS HEAD)

STRONG, CLEARLY DEFINED SHOULDERS

TORSO IS AVERAGE, BUT THE CHEST AND HIPS ARE EXAGGERATED

THICKER THIGHS AND CALVES, BUT KNEES AND ANKLES AVERAGE

CALVES MORE CLEARLY DEFINED

AMAZON

SHORT FIGURE, 4 HEADS TALL

ROUNDED, MINIMIZED SHOULDERS

ELBOWS SUNK INTO ARM, NOT STICKING OUT

WAIST HIGHER - THE TORSO, PELVIS AND LEGS ARE ROUGHLY EQUAL LENGTH

BENT ELBOW PART OF ONE BIG CURVE

BODY ALL CURVES, NO ANGLES

WRISTS AND ANKLES SAME THICKNESS AS AVERAGE FEMALE

AVERAGE TO SMALL HANDS AND FEET

HEAVY

THE SKELETON

WHAT YOU SEE OF THE HUMAN BODY IS REALLY JUST THE STUFF STRETCHED OVER AND AROUND THE SKELETON. SO LET'S TAKE A LOOK AT THE SKELETON AND HOW IT WORKS BEFORE DRAWING THE SURFACE OF THE FIGURE.

WHAT IS WHAT?
(CIRCLES SHOW PLACES WHERE THE BONES VISIBLY STICK OUT)

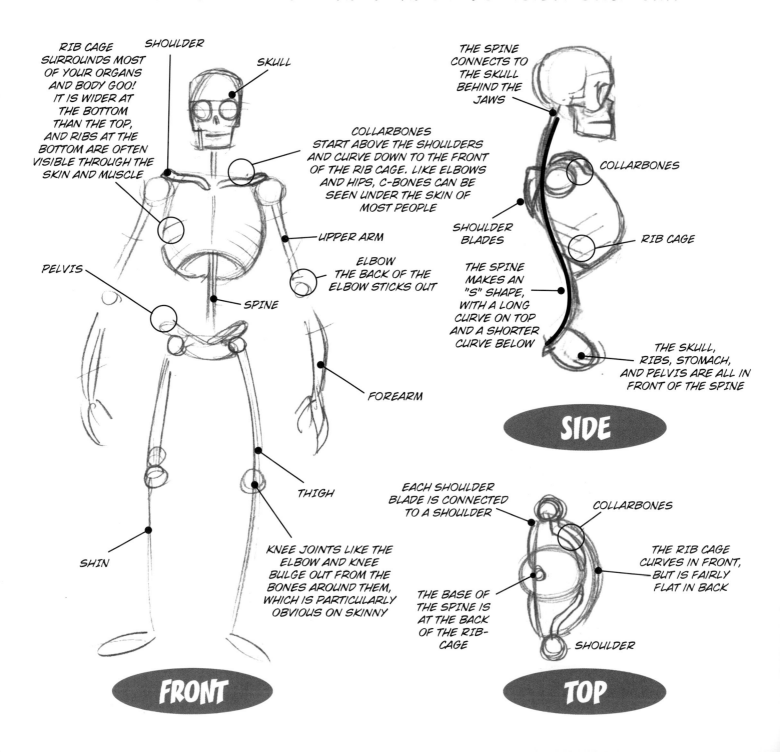

RIB CAGE SURROUNDS MOST OF YOUR ORGANS AND BODY GOO! IT IS WIDER AT THE BOTTOM THAN THE TOP, AND RIBS AT THE BOTTOM ARE OFTEN VISIBLE THROUGH THE SKIN AND MUSCLE

SHOULDER

SKULL

COLLARBONES START ABOVE THE SHOULDERS AND CURVE DOWN TO THE FRONT OF THE RIB CAGE. LIKE ELBOWS AND HIPS, C-BONES CAN BE SEEN UNDER THE SKIN OF MOST PEOPLE

UPPER ARM

ELBOW
THE BACK OF THE ELBOW STICKS OUT

PELVIS

SPINE

FOREARM

SHIN

THIGH

KNEE JOINTS LIKE THE ELBOW AND KNEE BULGE OUT FROM THE BONES AROUND THEM, WHICH IS PARTICULARLY OBVIOUS ON SKINNY

THE SPINE CONNECTS TO THE SKULL BEHIND THE JAWS

COLLARBONES

SHOULDER BLADES

RIB CAGE

THE SPINE MAKES AN "S" SHAPE, WITH A LONG CURVE ON TOP AND A SHORTER CURVE BELOW

THE SKULL, RIBS, STOMACH, AND PELVIS ARE ALL IN FRONT OF THE SPINE

SIDE

EACH SHOULDER BLADE IS CONNECTED TO A SHOULDER

COLLARBONES

THE RIB CAGE CURVES IN FRONT, BUT IS FAIRLY FLAT IN BACK

THE BASE OF THE SPINE IS AT THE BACK OF THE RIB-CAGE

SHOULDER

FRONT

TOP

SHOW A LITTLE BACKBONE

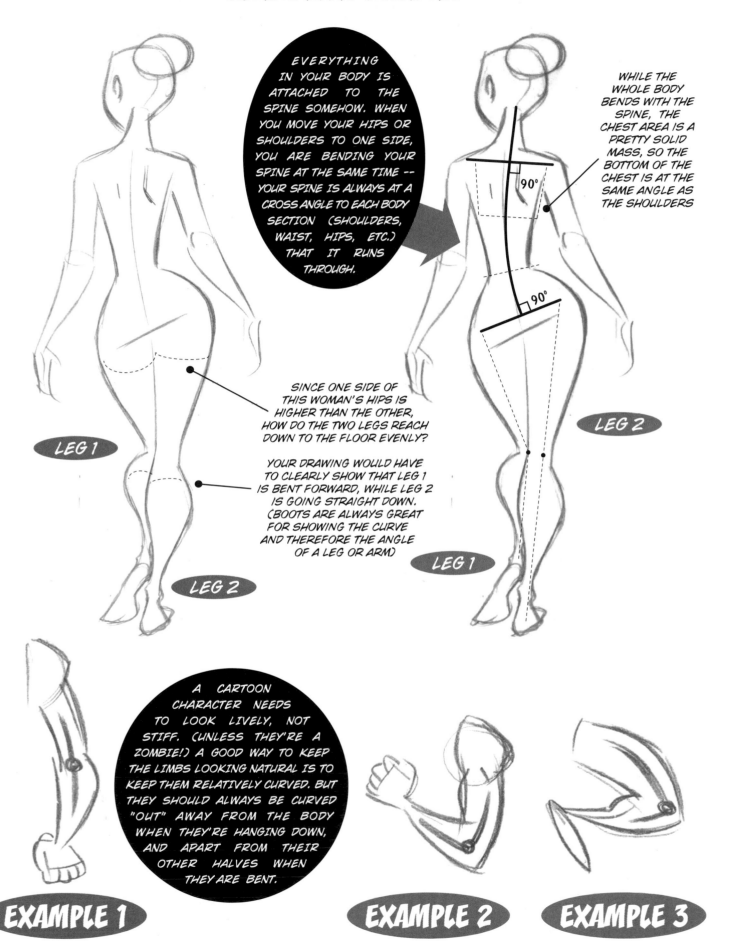

EVERYTHING IN YOUR BODY IS ATTACHED TO THE SPINE SOMEHOW. WHEN YOU MOVE YOUR HIPS OR SHOULDERS TO ONE SIDE, YOU ARE BENDING YOUR SPINE AT THE SAME TIME -- YOUR SPINE IS ALWAYS AT A CROSS ANGLE TO EACH BODY SECTION (SHOULDERS, WAIST, HIPS, ETC.) THAT IT RUNS THROUGH.

WHILE THE WHOLE BODY BENDS WITH THE SPINE, THE CHEST AREA IS A PRETTY SOLID MASS, SO THE BOTTOM OF THE CHEST IS AT THE SAME ANGLE AS THE SHOULDERS

90°

90°

LEG 2

SINCE ONE SIDE OF THIS WOMAN'S HIPS IS HIGHER THAN THE OTHER, HOW DO THE TWO LEGS REACH DOWN TO THE FLOOR EVENLY?

YOUR DRAWING WOULD HAVE TO CLEARLY SHOW THAT LEG 1 IS BENT FORWARD, WHILE LEG 2 IS GOING STRAIGHT DOWN. (BOOTS ARE ALWAYS GREAT FOR SHOWING THE CURVE AND THEREFORE THE ANGLE OF A LEG OR ARM)

LEG 1

LEG 1

LEG 2

A CARTOON CHARACTER NEEDS TO LOOK LIVELY, NOT STIFF. (UNLESS THEY'RE A ZOMBIE!) A GOOD WAY TO KEEP THE LIMBS LOOKING NATURAL IS TO KEEP THEM RELATIVELY CURVED. BUT THEY SHOULD ALWAYS BE CURVED "OUT" AWAY FROM THE BODY WHEN THEY'RE HANGING DOWN, AND APART FROM THEIR OTHER HALVES WHEN THEY ARE BENT.

EXAMPLE 1

EXAMPLE 2

EXAMPLE 3

THE TORSO

HERE ARE BASIC NOTES ON THE DETAILS OF THE TORSO AND HOW IT MOVES. THESE DETAILS ARE NOT ESPECIALLY CARTOONY, BUT CONCENTRATE ON SHOWING THE RAW INFORMATION OF THE BODY. ADD THIS INFORMATION TO THE CARTOONED PROPORTIONS YOU SAW IN THE GENERAL BODY SECTION (PAGES 36-41), AND YOU'RE GOOD TO GO!

BASIC FORMS AND PROPORTIONS

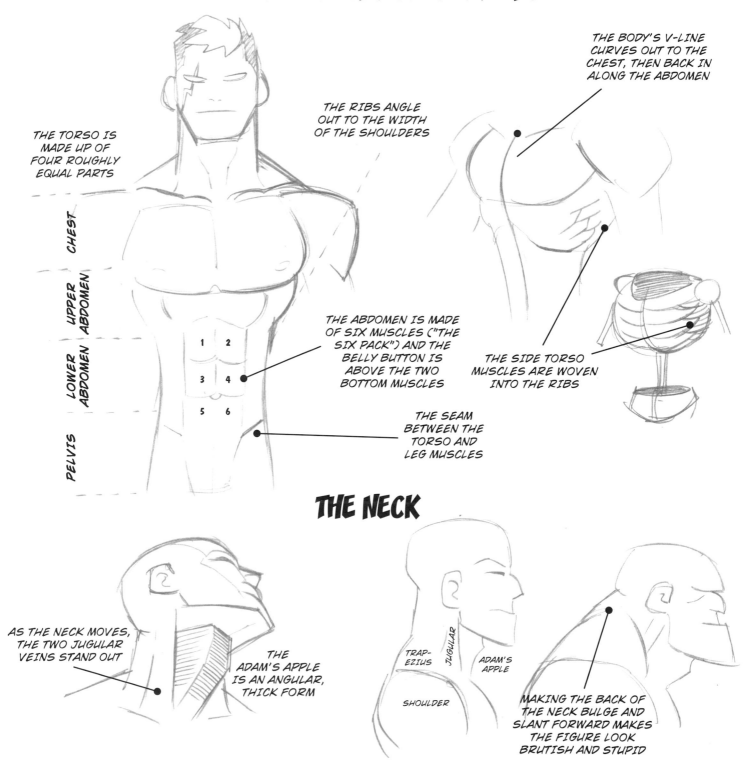

THE NECK

THE BACK

EXAMPLE 1

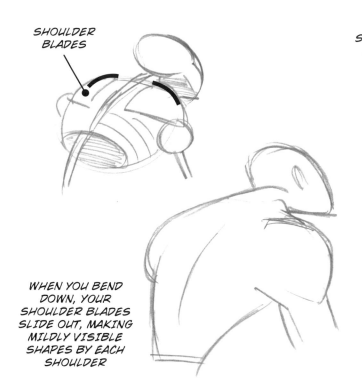

SHOULDER BLADES

WHEN YOU BEND DOWN, YOUR SHOULDER BLADES SLIDE OUT, MAKING MILDLY VISIBLE SHAPES BY EACH SHOULDER

EXAMPLE 2

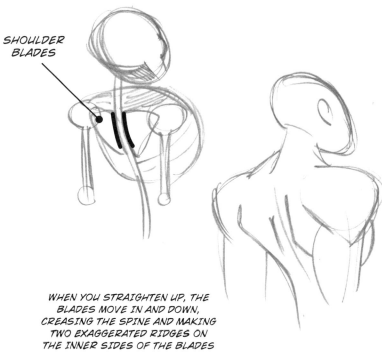

SHOULDER BLADES

WHEN YOU STRAIGHTEN UP, THE BLADES MOVE IN AND DOWN, CREASING THE SPINE AND MAKING TWO EXAGGERATED RIDGES ON THE INNER SIDES OF THE BLADES

THE STOMACH

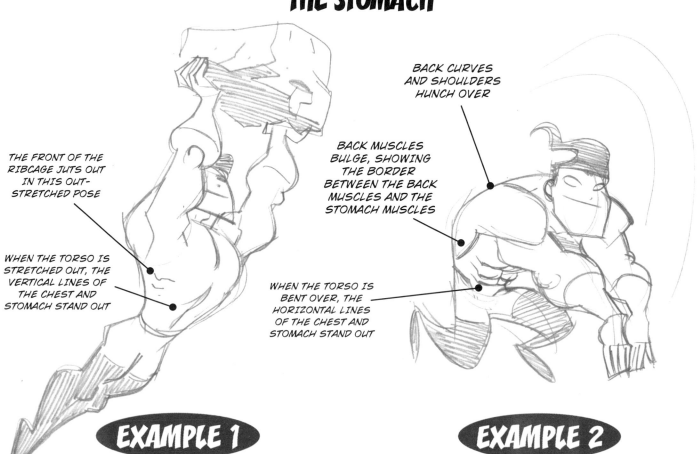

THE FRONT OF THE RIBCAGE JUTS OUT IN THIS OUT-STRETCHED POSE

WHEN THE TORSO IS STRETCHED OUT, THE VERTICAL LINES OF THE CHEST AND STOMACH STAND OUT

BACK CURVES AND SHOULDERS HUNCH OVER

BACK MUSCLES BULGE, SHOWING THE BORDER BETWEEN THE BACK MUSCLES AND THE STOMACH MUSCLES

WHEN THE TORSO IS BENT OVER, THE HORIZONTAL LINES OF THE CHEST AND STOMACH STAND OUT

EXAMPLE 1

EXAMPLE 2

THE ARMS

BASIC FORMS AND PROPORTIONS

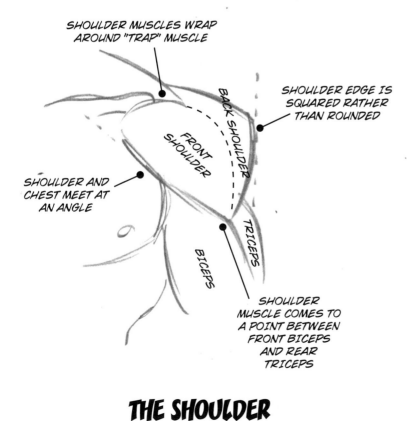

SHOULDER WIDEST PART OF ARM

SHOULDER TO ELBOWS SAME LENGTH AS ELBOWS TO WRIST

FROM THE FRONT, THE BICEPS MUSCLE LOOKS THIN, SINCE IT BULGES OUT AND NOT TO THE SIDES

FOREARM IS SECOND WIDEST PART OF ARM

FOREARM BULGES MORE NOTICEABLY IN INNER ARM

WRIST IS ABOUT HALF THE WIDTH OF FOREARM

MUSCLE CURVES

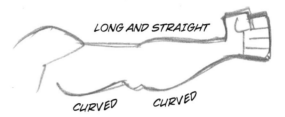

LONG AND STRAIGHT

CURVED   CURVED

SINCE ARMS HAVE A SLIGHT CURVE, WHEN THEY ARE STRAIGHTENED, THE OUTER SIDES BULGE MORE; WHEN ARMS ARE BENT, THE INNER SIDES BULGE. DON'T DRAW BOTH SIDES EQUALLY CURVED -- THEY'LL LOOK LIKE PUFFY MARSHMALLOWS!

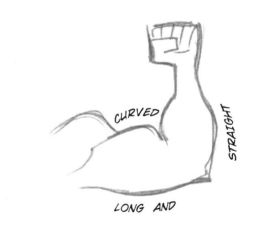

CURVED

STRAIGHT

LONG AND

SHOULDER MUSCLES WRAP AROUND "TRAP" MUSCLE

BACK SHOULDER

FRONT SHOULDER

SHOULDER EDGE IS SQUARED RATHER THAN ROUNDED

SHOULDER AND CHEST MEET AT AN ANGLE

TRICEPS

BICEPS

SHOULDER MUSCLE COMES TO A POINT BETWEEN FRONT BICEPS AND REAR TRICEPS

THE SHOULDER

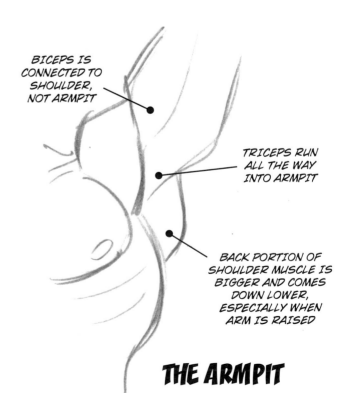

BICEPS IS CONNECTED TO SHOULDER, NOT ARMPIT

TRICEPS RUN ALL THE WAY INTO ARMPIT

BACK PORTION OF SHOULDER MUSCLE IS BIGGER AND COMES DOWN LOWER, ESPECIALLY WHEN ARM IS RAISED

THE ARMPIT

ARM MUSCLES

HERE ARE THE SPECIFIC ARM MUSCLES AND BONES UNDER THE SKIN. BELOW ARE ADDITIONAL ARM "POSES," SHOWING DIFFERENT ANGLES AND MOVEMENTS, AND MARKING HOW THE SAME MUSCLES AND BONES LOOK DIFFERENT UNDER DIFFERENT CIRCUMSTANCES.

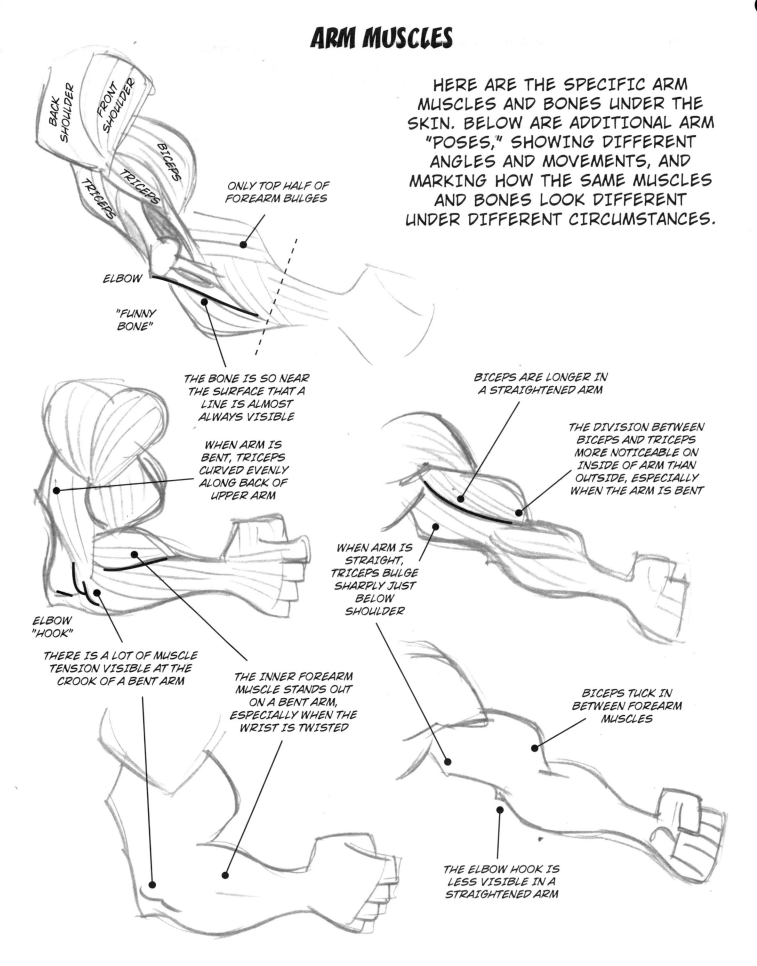

BACK SHOULDER

FRONT SHOULDER

BICEPS

TRICEPS

TRICEPS

ONLY TOP HALF OF FOREARM BULGES

ELBOW

"FUNNY BONE"

THE BONE IS SO NEAR THE SURFACE THAT A LINE IS ALMOST ALWAYS VISIBLE

WHEN ARM IS BENT, TRICEPS CURVED EVENLY ALONG BACK OF UPPER ARM

ELBOW "HOOK"

THERE IS A LOT OF MUSCLE TENSION VISIBLE AT THE CROOK OF A BENT ARM

THE INNER FOREARM MUSCLE STANDS OUT ON A BENT ARM, ESPECIALLY WHEN THE WRIST IS TWISTED

BICEPS ARE LONGER IN A STRAIGHTENED ARM

THE DIVISION BETWEEN BICEPS AND TRICEPS MORE NOTICEABLE ON INSIDE OF ARM THAN OUTSIDE, ESPECIALLY WHEN THE ARM IS BENT

WHEN ARM IS STRAIGHT, TRICEPS BULGE SHARPLY JUST BELOW SHOULDER

BICEPS TUCK IN BETWEEN FOREARM MUSCLES

THE ELBOW HOOK IS LESS VISIBLE IN A STRAIGHTENED ARM

THE HANDS

BASIC FORMS AND PROPORTIONS

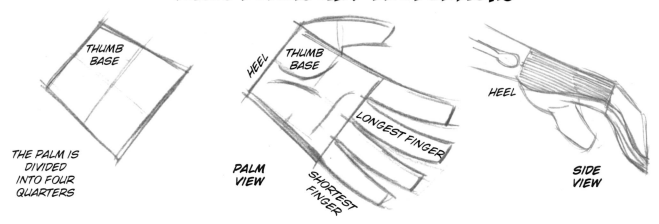

THUMB BASE

THE PALM IS DIVIDED INTO FOUR QUARTERS

HEEL

THUMB BASE

LONGEST FINGER

PALM VIEW

SHORTEST FINGER

HEEL

SIDE VIEW

KNUCKLES AND VEINS

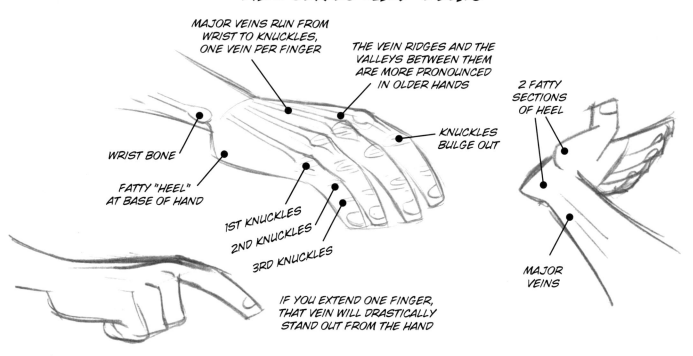

MAJOR VEINS RUN FROM WRIST TO KNUCKLES, ONE VEIN PER FINGER

THE VEIN RIDGES AND THE VALLEYS BETWEEN THEM ARE MORE PRONOUNCED IN OLDER HANDS

2 FATTY SECTIONS OF HEEL

KNUCKLES BULGE OUT

WRIST BONE

FATTY "HEEL" AT BASE OF HAND

1ST KNUCKLES

2ND KNUCKLES

3RD KNUCKLES

MAJOR VEINS

IF YOU EXTEND ONE FINGER, THAT VEIN WILL DRASTICALLY STAND OUT FROM THE HAND

NATURAL CURVE OF HAND

THE HAND HAS A NATURAL CURVE -- ONLY A CONSCIOUS EFFORT OR STRONG REACTION CAN CHANGE THE CURVE. THE MORE BENT BACK THE HANDS ARE, THE STRONGER THE EFFORT OR EMOTION THAT IS CAUSING THE MOVEMENT

STARTLED OR EXCITED

FINGERS

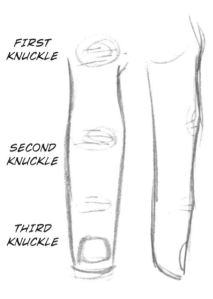

FIRST KNUCKLE

SECOND KNUCKLE

THIRD KNUCKLE

TOP VIEW

SIDE VIEW

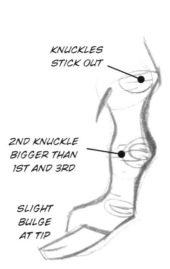

KNUCKLES STICK OUT

2ND KNUCKLE BIGGER THAN 1ST AND 3RD

SLIGHT BULGE AT TIP

GAUNT FINGER

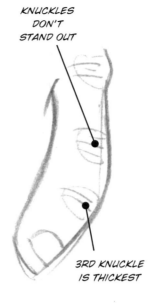

KNUCKLES DON'T STAND OUT

3RD KNUCKLE IS THICKEST

THICK FINGER

NORMAL OR SLENDER FINGERS (SIMPLIFIED)

STRONG OR BEEFY FINGERS (SIMPLIFIED)

THE FIST

FLAT

FLAT

FLAT

THE HIGH POINT OF THE FIST'S KNUCKLE RIDGE IS THE MIDDLE FINGER'S KNUCKLE

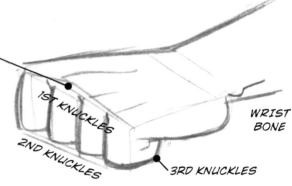

1ST KNUCKLES

2ND KNUCKLES

3RD KNUCKLES

WRIST BONE

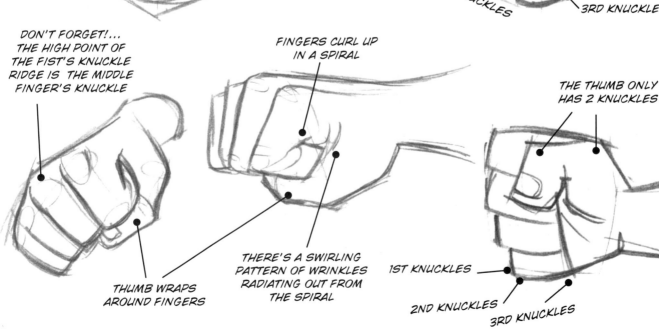

DON'T FORGET!... THE HIGH POINT OF THE FIST'S KNUCKLE RIDGE IS THE MIDDLE FINGER'S KNUCKLE

THUMB WRAPS AROUND FINGERS

FINGERS CURL UP IN A SPIRAL

THERE'S A SWIRLING PATTERN OF WRINKLES RADIATING OUT FROM THE SPIRAL

THE THUMB ONLY HAS 2 KNUCKLES

1ST KNUCKLES

2ND KNUCKLES

3RD KNUCKLES

THE LEGS

BASIC FORMS AND PROPORTIONS

LIKE THE ARMS, THE LEGS ARE AN ALTERNATING COMBINATION OF STRAIGHT AND CURVED LINES

OUTER PARTS OF LEG ARE HIGHER THAN INNER PARTS

THICKEST PART OF LEG 1/2 WAY DOWN UPPER LEG

THIGH MUSCLE

2 MAJOR FRONT LEG MUSCLES SPLIT TO EACH SIDE OF THE KNEE

KNEE 1/2 WAY FROM HIP TO ANKLE

KNEE MUSCLES CONTINUE INTO LOWER LEG BONE

LOWER LEG BULGES MORE ON INSIDE THAN OUTSIDE

LIKE THE FOREARM, LOWER LEG THINS BELOW 1/2 WAY POINT

ANKLE NARROWER THAN KNEE

LOWER LEGS

WHEN THE LEGS ARE TIGHTLY TOGETHER, THEY NARROW TO A POINT

THE CALF MUSCLES SLIP IN BETWEEN THE UPPER LEG MUSCLES

LOWER PARTS OF THE CALF STAND OUT ON THE SIDES WHEN THE FOOT IS EXTENDED

THERE ARE 2 CALF MUSCLES

THE CALF MUSCLES WRAP AROUND THE LOWER LEG

WHEN THE FOOT IS EXTENDED DOWN, THE CALF MUSCLES BULGE OUT

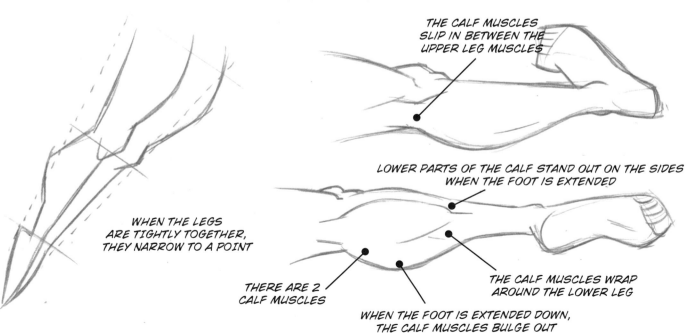

KNEES

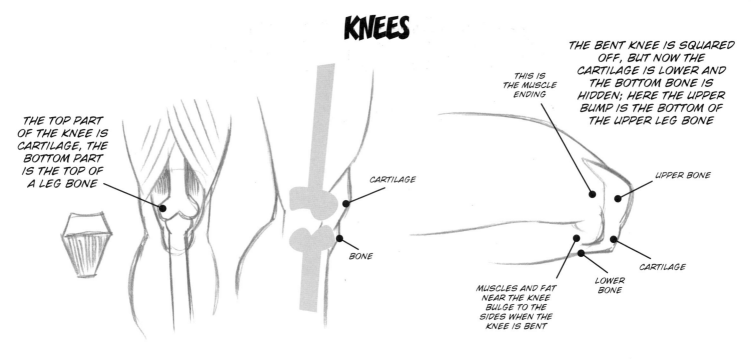

THE TOP PART OF THE KNEE IS CARTILAGE, THE BOTTOM PART IS THE TOP OF A LEG BONE

THIS IS THE MUSCLE ENDING

CARTILAGE

BONE

THE BENT KNEE IS SQUARED OFF, BUT NOW THE CARTILAGE IS LOWER AND THE BOTTOM BONE IS HIDDEN; HERE THE UPPER BUMP IS THE BOTTOM OF THE UPPER LEG BONE

UPPER BONE

CARTILAGE

LOWER BONE

MUSCLES AND FAT NEAR THE KNEE BULGE TO THE SIDES WHEN THE KNEE IS BENT

FEET

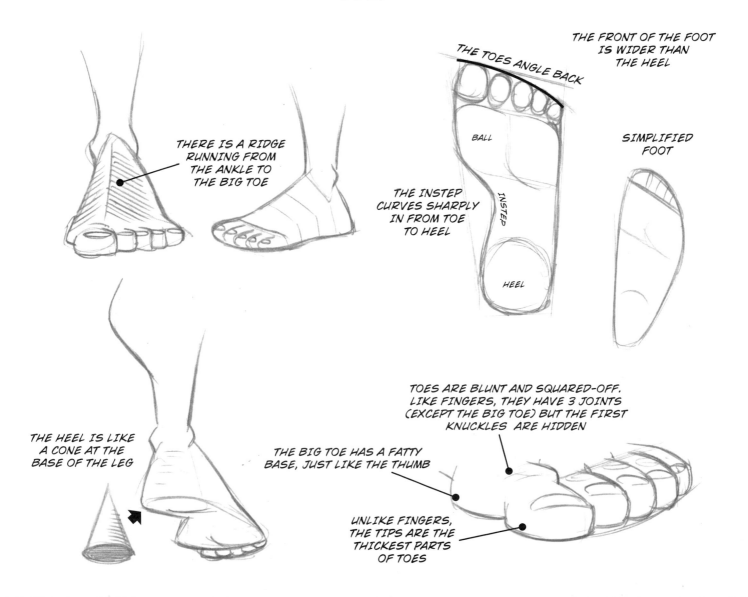

THERE IS A RIDGE RUNNING FROM THE ANKLE TO THE BIG TOE

THE TOES ANGLE BACK

THE FRONT OF THE FOOT IS WIDER THAN THE HEEL

BALL

SIMPLIFIED FOOT

THE INSTEP CURVES SHARPLY IN FROM TOE TO HEEL

INSTEP

HEEL

THE HEEL IS LIKE A CONE AT THE BASE OF THE LEG

THE BIG TOE HAS A FATTY BASE, JUST LIKE THE THUMB

TOES ARE BLUNT AND SQUARED-OFF. LIKE FINGERS, THEY HAVE 3 JOINTS (EXCEPT THE BIG TOE) BUT THE FIRST KNUCKLES ARE HIDDEN

UNLIKE FINGERS, THE TIPS ARE THE THICKEST PARTS OF TOES

ACTION POSES!

THIS IS WHAT YOU'VE BEEN WAITING FOR --
STEP-BY-STEP EXAMPLES OF CARTOON CHARACTERS
AND POSES FOR YOU TO DRAW! WE'LL BRIEFLY TALK
ABOUT MAKING EACH POSE AS ACTION-PACKED AS
POSSIBLE, THEN SEE HOW TO BUILD ROUGH
SKELETONS INTO FULLY DEVELOPED ALL-
OUT ACTION POSES!

ACTION BASICS

BEFORE WE START DRAWING POSES, HERE ARE SUGGESTIONS FOR GETTING THE MOST DRAMA OUT OF YOUR DRAWINGS. BY CHANGING YOUR POINT OF VIEW TO LOOK AT THE SCENE FROM ABOVE (OR BELOW, OR "OVER-THE-SHOULDER"), OR EXAGGERATING A CHARACTER'S STANCE OR MUSCLE TENSION, YOU CAN ADD A GREATER SENSE OF ACTION TO YOUR ACTION SCENES!

CHANGING VIEWS

EXAMPLE 1

THIS CHARACTER IS LOOKING AT SOMETHING OFF THE PAGE. SINCE HIS BODY IS SO STATIC, WE CAN'T TELL IF HE'S LOOKING AT A MONSTER OR A JAR OF MAYONNAISE

EXAMPLE 2

BY TURNING HIS HEAD IN A DIFFERENT DIRECTION THAN HIS BODY, YOU SUGGEST THAT THIS CHARACTER HAS STOPPED WHAT HE WAS DOING TO LOOK AT THE SOMETHING OFF THE PAGE. SO WHATEVER IT IS, WE NOW KNOW THAT IT IS INTERESTING ENOUGH TO GRAB THIS GUY'S ATTENTION

EXAMPLE 3

THIS IS JUST A MORE EXTREME VERSION OF POSE 2. HIS OVER-THE-SHOULDER LOOK SUGGESTS THAT THE OFF-PAGE "SOMETHING" IS RIGHT BEHIND HIM... READY TO STRIKE!

IN THESE FINAL TWO EXAMPLES YOU CAN SEE HOW LOOKING UP OR DOWN AT THE FIGURE OFTEN MAKES THE SCENE/POSE LOOK MORE DRAMATIC

EXAGGERATED STANCE

SOMETIMES THE EASIEST WAY TO PUMP UP THE ACTION IN FIGURES IS TO EXAGGERATE THEIR STANCE OR MOTION -- IF THEY ARE STANDING, THEIR LEGS AND ARMS COULD BE FARTHER APART FROM THE BODY, IF THEY ARE WALKING, THEY COULD TAKE LONGER STEPS AND SWING THEIR ARMS OUT IN FRONT AND BACK OF THEM. BY TAKING UP EXTRA SPACE, SUCH FIGURES WILL DOMINATE A PAGE AND OVERWHELM OTHER FIGURES. THEY WILL ALSO LOOK MORE SOLIDLY BALANCED AND GROUNDED, WHICH MAKES THEM LOOK STRONGER.

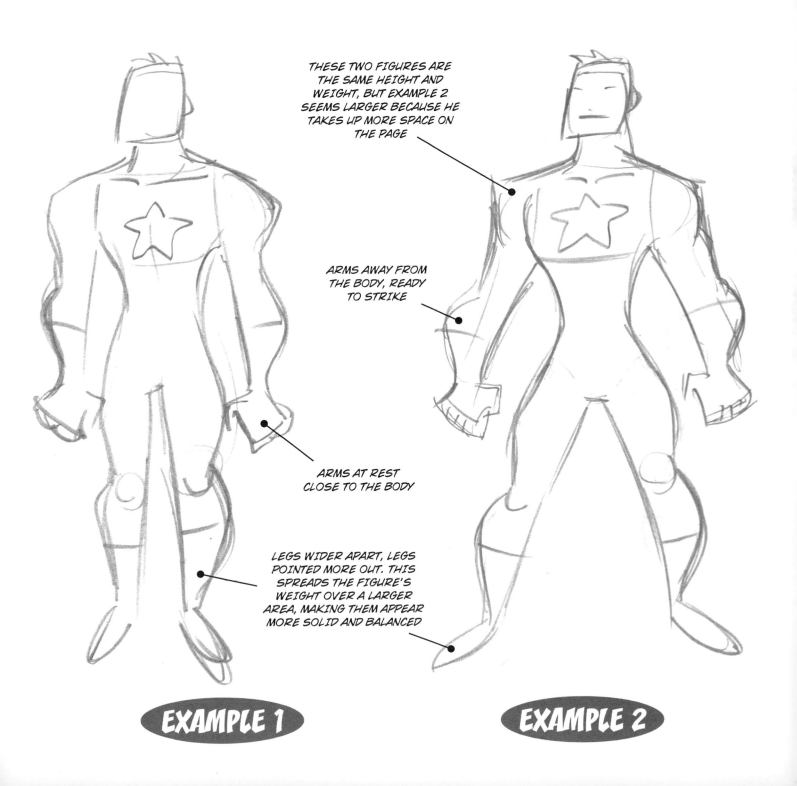

THESE TWO FIGURES ARE THE SAME HEIGHT AND WEIGHT, BUT EXAMPLE 2 SEEMS LARGER BECAUSE HE TAKES UP MORE SPACE ON THE PAGE

ARMS AWAY FROM THE BODY, READY TO STRIKE

ARMS AT REST CLOSE TO THE BODY

LEGS WIDER APART, LEGS POINTED MORE OUT. THIS SPREADS THE FIGURE'S WEIGHT OVER A LARGER AREA, MAKING THEM APPEAR MORE SOLID AND BALANCED

EXAMPLE 1

EXAMPLE 2

EXAGGERATED ACTION

LOOK AT THE DIFFERENCE BETWEEN A PUNCH AND AN *ACTION* PUNCH!

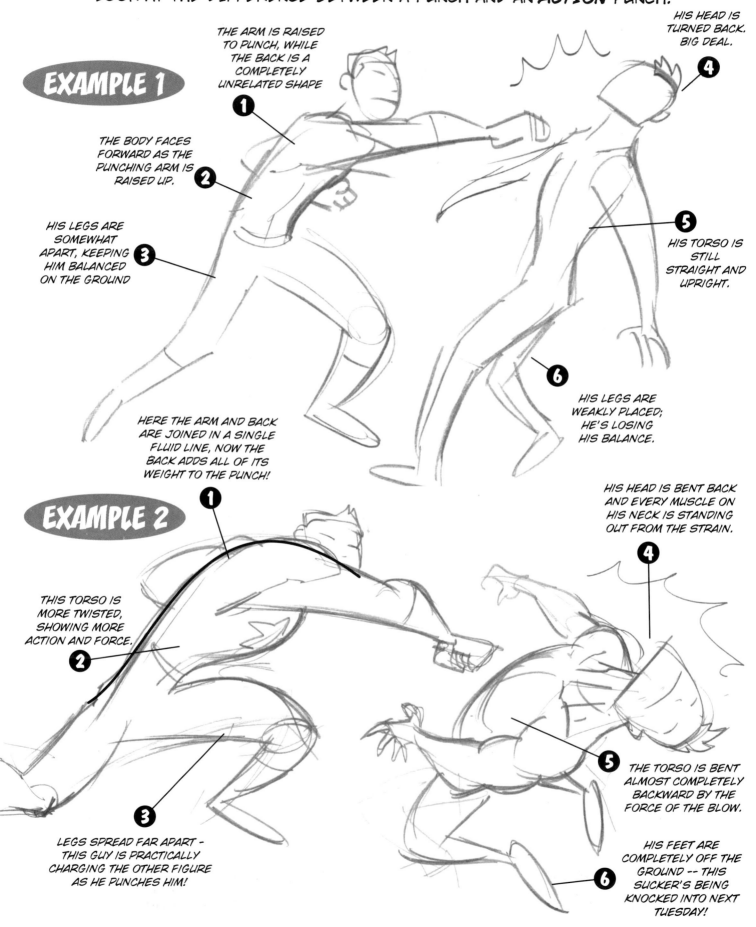

EXAMPLE 1

THE ARM IS RAISED TO PUNCH, WHILE THE BACK IS A COMPLETELY UNRELATED SHAPE ①

THE BODY FACES FORWARD AS THE PUNCHING ARM IS RAISED UP. ②

HIS LEGS ARE SOMEWHAT APART, KEEPING HIM BALANCED ON THE GROUND ③

HIS HEAD IS TURNED BACK. BIG DEAL. ④

HIS TORSO IS STILL STRAIGHT AND UPRIGHT. ⑤

HIS LEGS ARE WEAKLY PLACED; HE'S LOSING HIS BALANCE. ⑥

HERE THE ARM AND BACK ARE JOINED IN A SINGLE FLUID LINE, NOW THE BACK ADDS ALL OF ITS WEIGHT TO THE PUNCH! ①

EXAMPLE 2

THIS TORSO IS MORE TWISTED, SHOWING MORE ACTION AND FORCE. ②

LEGS SPREAD FAR APART - THIS GUY IS PRACTICALLY CHARGING THE OTHER FIGURE AS HE PUNCHES HIM! ③

HIS HEAD IS BENT BACK AND EVERY MUSCLE ON HIS NECK IS STANDING OUT FROM THE STRAIN. ④

THE TORSO IS BENT ALMOST COMPLETELY BACKWARD BY THE FORCE OF THE BLOW. ⑤

HIS FEET ARE COMPLETELY OFF THE GROUND -- THIS SUCKER'S BEING KNOCKED INTO NEXT TUESDAY! ⑥

HERE IS **ATALANTA**, THE FASTEST RUNNER IN ANCIENT GREECE. EXAMPLE 1 IS WHAT AN ACCURATE PHOTO OF HER MOVEMENT WOULD LOOK LIKE, BUT EXAMPLE 2 SHOWS HOW THE ACTION ACTUALLY FEELS TO BOTH ATALANTA AND THE VIEWER. LIMBS ARE FARTHER AWAY FROM THE BODY AND THE WHOLE BODY IS LEANING INTO HER MOTION

EXAMPLE 1

EXAMPLE 2

RED RAZOR MAY LOOK A LITTLE SURPRISED IN EXAMPLE 1, BUT IN EXAMPLE 2 YOU CAN FEEL HIS SURPRISE FROM A MILE AWAY! ONCE AGAIN, THE LIMBS ARE FARTHER AWAY FROM THE TORSO; AND THERE IS MORE TENSION BETWEEN THE TORSO FACING ONE WAY AND THE NECK AND HEAD TWISTING IN ANOTHER

EXAMPLE 1

EXAMPLE 2

A FEW MORE HINTS

NOW THAT YOU KNOW THE ACTION BASICS, HERE ARE SOME TIPS FOR MAKING YOUR FIGURES LOOK SOLID USING *FORESHORTENING*, *OVERLAPPING*, AND *CONTOURS*.

FORESHORTENING

FORESHORTENING IS A TRICK TO MAKE OBJECTS LOOK LIKE THEY ARE RELATIVELY NEAR OR FAR FROM YOU. IT ALSO HELPS TO SHOW THE *VOLUME* OF AN OBJECT -- THE SURFACE CURVES THAT MAKE THE OBJECT SEEM TO TAKE UP SPACE.

HERE ARE TWO VIEWS OF THE SAME CAN. AS ITS TOP IS TURNED TOWARD YOU, MORE OF THE TOP AND LESS OF THE SIDE IS VISIBLE. AT THE SAME TIME, THE SURFACE CURVE OF THE CAN BECOMES MORE ROUNDED AND OBVIOUS, AND ANY IMAGES OR FLAT OBJECTS ON THE SIDE OF THE CAN WILL ALSO LOOK MORE CURVED.

IT'S JUST A SMALL STEP TO CHANGE BASIC SHAPES INTO THE MORE COMPLEX SHAPES OF THE BODY. JUST REMEMBER THAT LINES GET SHORTER AND CURVES MORE PRONOUNCED AS AN OBJECT IS FORESHORTENED. THE NEXT STEP TO MAKING A FORESHORTENED OBJECT LOOK BELIEVABLY ROUND IS OVERLAPPING LINES, LIKE THOSE ON THE FORESHORTENED ARM BELOW.

OF COURSE, YOU DIDN'T BUY THIS BOOK TO DRAW CANS! BUT YOU CAN "BUILD" BODY PARTS OUT OF BASIC SHAPES LIKE TUBES AND SPHERES. THIS IS A GREAT WAY TO WORK OUT THE FORESHORTENING OF LIMBS, ETC.

OVERLAPPING

OVERLAPPING LINES ON A DRAWING SHOW WHAT OBJECTS ARE IN FRONT OF OTHERS. THEY ALSO HELP TO SHOW THE SURFACE CURVE OF AN OBJECT. OVERLAPPING LINES ARE MOST OFTEN FOUND AT THE PARTS OF THE BODY THAT, ON THE PREVIOUS PAGE, WERE SHOWN AS THE JOINTS BETWEEN THE DIFFERENT TUBES AND CUBES AND SPHERES OF THE FORESHORTENED ARM. THE MORE FORESHORTENED AN OBJECT IS, THE MORE OVERLAPPING LINES WILL DIVIDE IT FROM ITS NEIGHBORING PARTS.

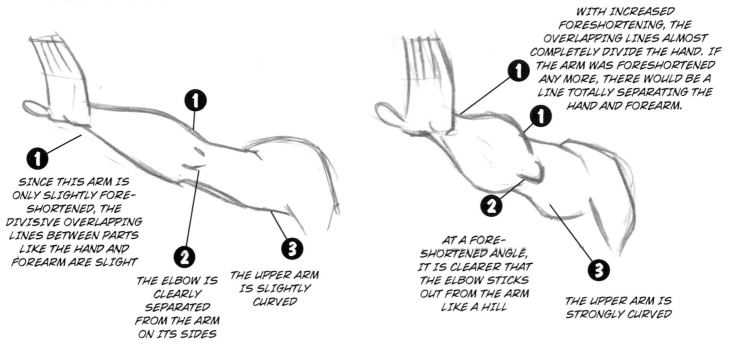

WITH INCREASED FORESHORTENING, THE OVERLAPPING LINES ALMOST COMPLETELY DIVIDE THE HAND. IF THE ARM WAS FORESHORTENED ANY MORE, THERE WOULD BE A LINE TOTALLY SEPARATING THE HAND AND FOREARM.

SINCE THIS ARM IS ONLY SLIGHTLY FORE-SHORTENED, THE DIVISIVE OVERLAPPING LINES BETWEEN PARTS LIKE THE HAND AND FOREARM ARE SLIGHT

THE ELBOW IS CLEARLY SEPARATED FROM THE ARM ON ITS SIDES

THE UPPER ARM IS SLIGHTLY CURVED

AT A FORE-SHORTENED ANGLE, IT IS CLEARER THAT THE ELBOW STICKS OUT FROM THE ARM LIKE A HILL

THE UPPER ARM IS STRONGLY CURVED

OVERLAPPING IS ALSO ESSENTIAL WHEN OBJECTS ARE PRESSED TOGETHER -- AFTER ALL, ALMOST NOTHING LINES UP PERFECTLY IN NATURE, SO SOMETHING HAS TO BE CLOSER OR FARTHER, HIGHER OR LOWER ETC. THIS SORT OF OVERLAPPING IS WHAT WE DRAW FOR MUSCLE BULGES AND CREASES IN BODY PARTS.

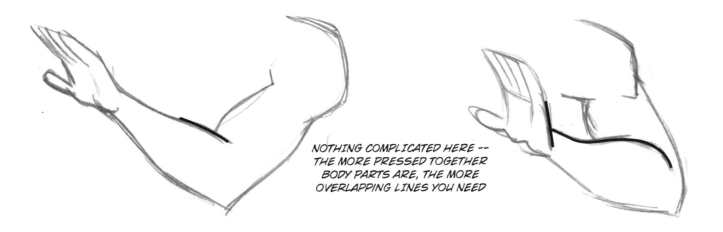

NOTHING COMPLICATED HERE -- THE MORE PRESSED TOGETHER BODY PARTS ARE, THE MORE OVERLAPPING LINES YOU NEED

SO ENOUGH WITH THE SMALL TALK -- IT'S TIME TO DRAW!

WALK 1

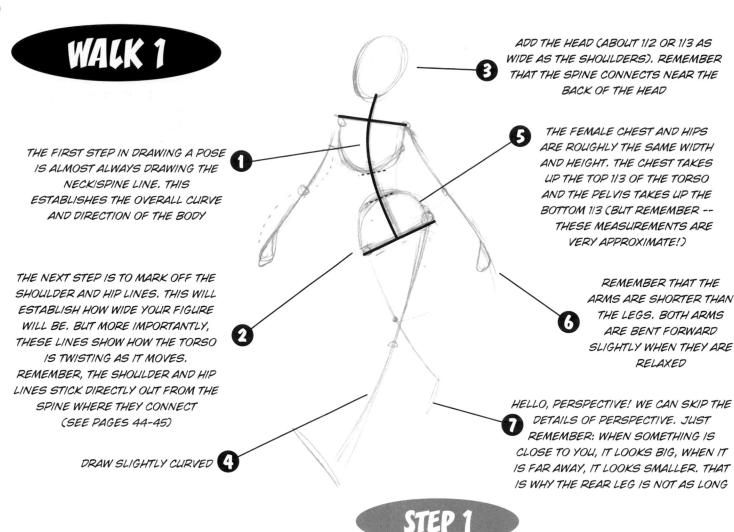

1 THE FIRST STEP IN DRAWING A POSE IS ALMOST ALWAYS DRAWING THE NECK/SPINE LINE. THIS ESTABLISHES THE OVERALL CURVE AND DIRECTION OF THE BODY

2 THE NEXT STEP IS TO MARK OFF THE SHOULDER AND HIP LINES. THIS WILL ESTABLISH HOW WIDE YOUR FIGURE WILL BE. BUT MORE IMPORTANTLY, THESE LINES SHOW HOW THE TORSO IS TWISTING AS IT MOVES. REMEMBER, THE SHOULDER AND HIP LINES STICK DIRECTLY OUT FROM THE SPINE WHERE THEY CONNECT (SEE PAGES 44-45)

4 DRAW SLIGHTLY CURVED

3 ADD THE HEAD (ABOUT 1/2 OR 1/3 AS WIDE AS THE SHOULDERS). REMEMBER THAT THE SPINE CONNECTS NEAR THE BACK OF THE HEAD

5 THE FEMALE CHEST AND HIPS ARE ROUGHLY THE SAME WIDTH AND HEIGHT. THE CHEST TAKES UP THE TOP 1/3 OF THE TORSO AND THE PELVIS TAKES UP THE BOTTOM 1/3 (BUT REMEMBER -- THESE MEASUREMENTS ARE VERY APPROXIMATE!)

6 REMEMBER THAT THE ARMS ARE SHORTER THAN THE LEGS. BOTH ARMS ARE BENT FORWARD SLIGHTLY WHEN THEY ARE RELAXED

7 HELLO, PERSPECTIVE! WE CAN SKIP THE DETAILS OF PERSPECTIVE. JUST REMEMBER: WHEN SOMETHING IS CLOSE TO YOU, IT LOOKS BIG, WHEN IT IS FAR AWAY, IT LOOKS SMALLER. THAT IS WHY THE REAR LEG IS NOT AS LONG

STEP 1

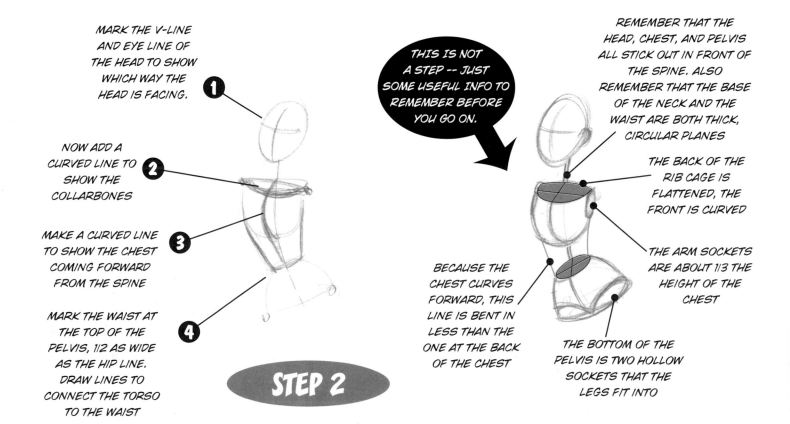

1 MARK THE V-LINE AND EYE LINE OF THE HEAD TO SHOW WHICH WAY THE HEAD IS FACING.

2 NOW ADD A CURVED LINE TO SHOW THE COLLARBONES

3 MAKE A CURVED LINE TO SHOW THE CHEST COMING FORWARD FROM THE SPINE

4 MARK THE WAIST AT THE TOP OF THE PELVIS, 1/2 AS WIDE AS THE HIP LINE. DRAW LINES TO CONNECT THE TORSO TO THE WAIST

THIS IS NOT A STEP -- JUST SOME USEFUL INFO TO REMEMBER BEFORE YOU GO ON.

REMEMBER THAT THE HEAD, CHEST, AND PELVIS ALL STICK OUT IN FRONT OF THE SPINE. ALSO REMEMBER THAT THE BASE OF THE NECK AND THE WAIST ARE BOTH THICK, CIRCULAR PLANES

THE BACK OF THE RIB CAGE IS FLATTENED, THE FRONT IS CURVED

THE ARM SOCKETS ARE ABOUT 1/3 THE HEIGHT OF THE CHEST

BECAUSE THE CHEST CURVES FORWARD, THIS LINE IS BENT IN LESS THAN THE ONE AT THE BACK OF THE CHEST

THE BOTTOM OF THE PELVIS IS TWO HOLLOW SOCKETS THAT THE LEGS FIT INTO

STEP 2

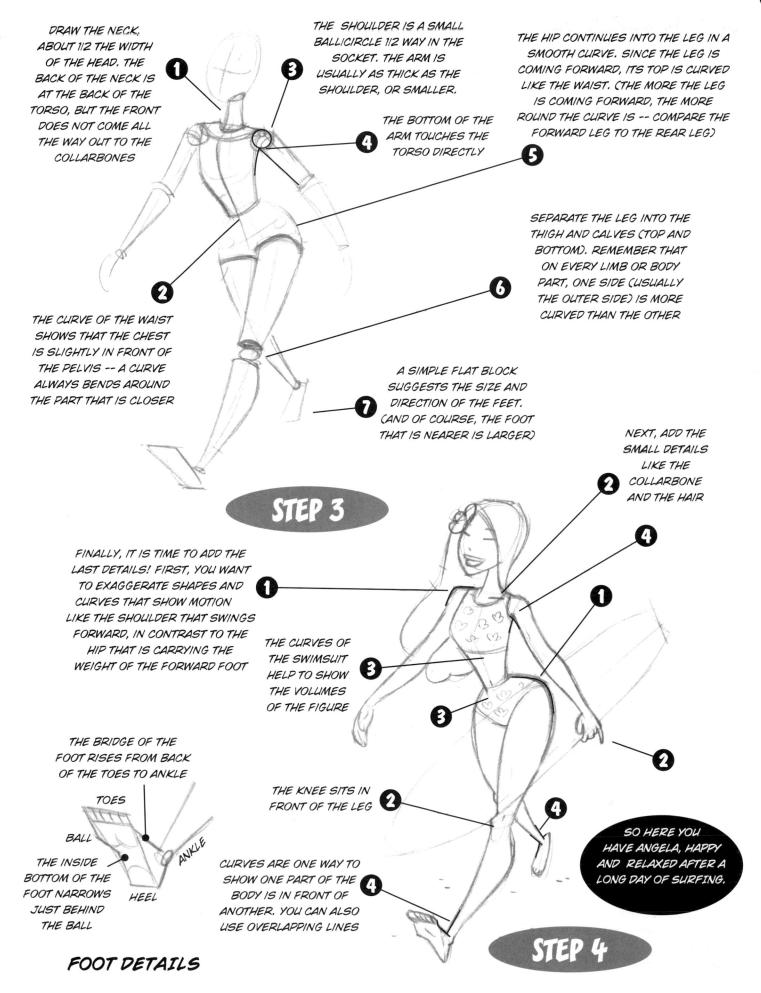

DRAW THE NECK, ABOUT 1/2 THE WIDTH OF THE HEAD. THE BACK OF THE NECK IS AT THE BACK OF THE TORSO, BUT THE FRONT DOES NOT COME ALL THE WAY OUT TO THE COLLARBONES

THE SHOULDER IS A SMALL BALL/CIRCLE 1/2 WAY IN THE SOCKET. THE ARM IS USUALLY AS THICK AS THE SHOULDER, OR SMALLER.

THE HIP CONTINUES INTO THE LEG IN A SMOOTH CURVE. SINCE THE LEG IS COMING FORWARD, ITS TOP IS CURVED LIKE THE WAIST. (THE MORE THE LEG IS COMING FORWARD, THE MORE ROUND THE CURVE IS -- COMPARE THE FORWARD LEG TO THE REAR LEG)

THE BOTTOM OF THE ARM TOUCHES THE TORSO DIRECTLY

SEPARATE THE LEG INTO THE THIGH AND CALVES (TOP AND BOTTOM). REMEMBER THAT ON EVERY LIMB OR BODY PART, ONE SIDE (USUALLY THE OUTER SIDE) IS MORE CURVED THAN THE OTHER

THE CURVE OF THE WAIST SHOWS THAT THE CHEST IS SLIGHTLY IN FRONT OF THE PELVIS -- A CURVE ALWAYS BENDS AROUND THE PART THAT IS CLOSER

A SIMPLE FLAT BLOCK SUGGESTS THE SIZE AND DIRECTION OF THE FEET. (AND OF COURSE, THE FOOT THAT IS NEARER IS LARGER)

STEP 3

NEXT, ADD THE SMALL DETAILS LIKE THE COLLARBONE AND THE HAIR

FINALLY, IT IS TIME TO ADD THE LAST DETAILS! FIRST, YOU WANT TO EXAGGERATE SHAPES AND CURVES THAT SHOW MOTION LIKE THE SHOULDER THAT SWINGS FORWARD, IN CONTRAST TO THE HIP THAT IS CARRYING THE WEIGHT OF THE FORWARD FOOT

THE CURVES OF THE SWIMSUIT HELP TO SHOW THE VOLUMES OF THE FIGURE

THE BRIDGE OF THE FOOT RISES FROM BACK OF THE TOES TO ANKLE

TOES

BALL

ANKLE

THE INSIDE BOTTOM OF THE FOOT NARROWS JUST BEHIND THE BALL

HEEL

THE KNEE SITS IN FRONT OF THE LEG

CURVES ARE ONE WAY TO SHOW ONE PART OF THE BODY IS IN FRONT OF ANOTHER. YOU CAN ALSO USE OVERLAPPING LINES

SO HERE YOU HAVE ANGELA, HAPPY AND RELAXED AFTER A LONG DAY OF SURFING.

STEP 4

FOOT DETAILS

WALK 2

IN THIS POSE, YOU'LL SEE HOW CHANGING THE ANGLE OF THE SHOULDERS, NECK ETC. CAN CHANGE THE ATTITUDE OF A CHARACTER. THIS POSE IS VERY SIMILAR TO WALK 1, BUT A FEW CHANGES REVEAL A COMPLETELY DIFFERENT PERSONALITY!

NOW ADD THE SHOULDER AND HIP LINES. FOR THIS MALE FIGURE, THE HIPS ARE ABOUT HALF THE WIDTH OF THE SHOULDERS

MAKING THE SHOULDERS AND HIPS SO NEATLY PARALLEL MAKES THE FIGURE LOOK STIFF. USUALLY THAT'S A BAD THING, BUT WE WANT THIS PARTICULAR POSE TO LOOK STIFF AND TENSE

DRAW THE LEGS. THEY ARE SLIGHTLY CURVED LIKE WALK 1, BUT SPREAD OUT MUCH FURTHER, SUGGESTING A MORE AGGRESSIVE WALK

START WITH A FORWARD LEANING SPINE

FILL OUT THE CHEST AND HIPS, ADD THE HEAD. SINCE THE NECK IS STICKING FORWARD, REMEMBER THAT THE NECK DOES NOT CONNECT TO THE BOTTOM OF THE HEAD, BUT TO THE REAR

DRAW THE ARMS. SINCE THIS FIGURE IS TENSE, THE ARMS ARE NOT SWINGING FREELY, BUT HANGING DOWN WITH THE ELBOWS OUT -- LIKE A MAD GORILLA!

STEP 1

MARK THE V-LINE AND EYE LINE OF THE HEAD, TO SHOW WHICH WAY THE HEAD IS FACING

NOW ADD A CURVED LINE TO SHOW THE COLLARBONES, AND ANOTHER TO SHOW THE TOP OF THE TORSO

MAKE A CURVED LINE TO SHOW THE CHEST COMING FORWARD FROM THE SPINE. ALSO MARK OFF THE BOTTOM OF THE CHEST (THE CHEST IS THE TOP THIRD OF THE TORSO)

MARK THE WAIST AT THE TOP OF THE PELVIS, ABOUT AS WIDE AS THE HIP LINE. DRAW LINES TO CONNECT THE TORSO TO THE WAIST

THE NECK IS SO THICK THAT IT BULGES OUT. IT ALSO COMES DOWN TO THE COLLARBONES IN FRONT

FOR THIS MUSCULAR FELLOW, MAKE THE SHOULDERS AS DEEP AS THE CHEST

THE ARMS ARE SLIGHTLY THINNER THAN THE SHOULDER. THEY NARROW DOWN TO OVERSIZED, SQUARED-OFF HANDS. NOTE THAT EVEN WHEN THE ARMS ARE STRAIGHT AND STIFF, THEY STILL HAVE A LITTLE CURVE TO THEM

THE CALVES AND FEET ARE EXAGGERATED TO SHOW THE ENERGY OF THE WALK. ON EACH BODY PART, ONE SIDE IS ALWAYS MORE CURVED THAN THE OTHER

STEP 2

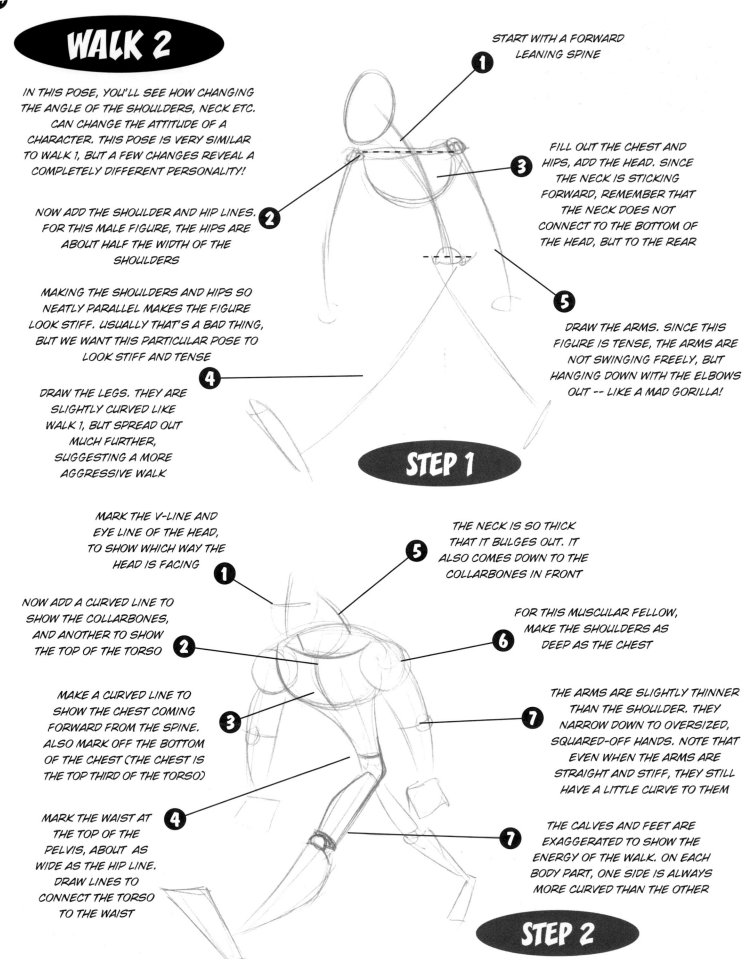

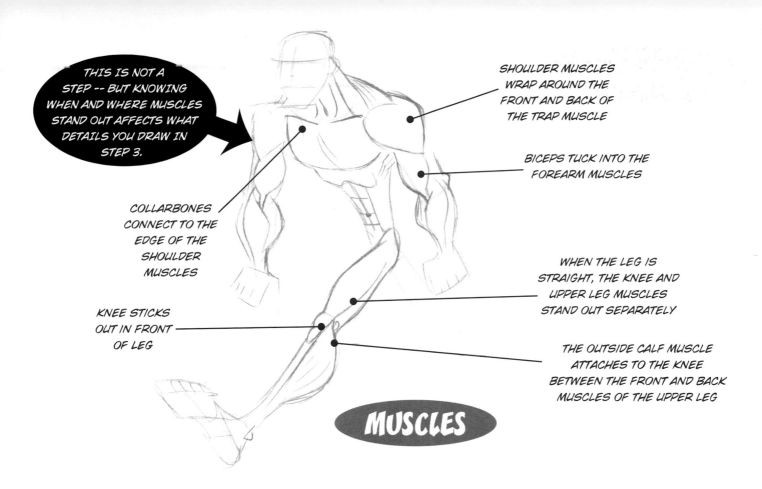

THIS IS NOT A STEP -- BUT KNOWING WHEN AND WHERE MUSCLES STAND OUT AFFECTS WHAT DETAILS YOU DRAW IN STEP 3.

SHOULDER MUSCLES WRAP AROUND THE FRONT AND BACK OF THE TRAP MUSCLE

BICEPS TUCK INTO THE FOREARM MUSCLES

COLLARBONES CONNECT TO THE EDGE OF THE SHOULDER MUSCLES

WHEN THE LEG IS STRAIGHT, THE KNEE AND UPPER LEG MUSCLES STAND OUT SEPARATELY

KNEE STICKS OUT IN FRONT OF LEG

THE OUTSIDE CALF MUSCLE ATTACHES TO THE KNEE BETWEEN THE FRONT AND BACK MUSCLES OF THE UPPER LEG

MUSCLES

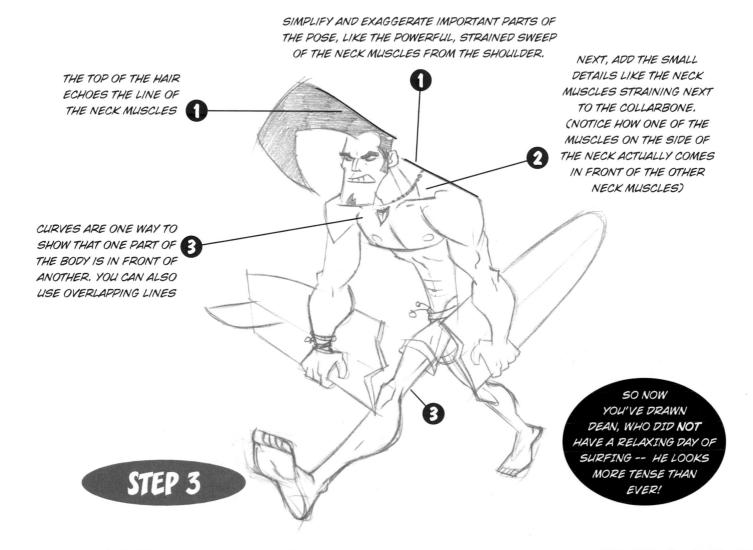

SIMPLIFY AND EXAGGERATE IMPORTANT PARTS OF THE POSE, LIKE THE POWERFUL, STRAINED SWEEP OF THE NECK MUSCLES FROM THE SHOULDER.

NEXT, ADD THE SMALL DETAILS LIKE THE NECK MUSCLES STRAINING NEXT TO THE COLLARBONE. (NOTICE HOW ONE OF THE MUSCLES ON THE SIDE OF THE NECK ACTUALLY COMES IN FRONT OF THE OTHER NECK MUSCLES)

THE TOP OF THE HAIR ECHOES THE LINE OF THE NECK MUSCLES

CURVES ARE ONE WAY TO SHOW THAT ONE PART OF THE BODY IS IN FRONT OF ANOTHER. YOU CAN ALSO USE OVERLAPPING LINES

SO NOW YOU'VE DRAWN DEAN, WHO DID **NOT** HAVE A RELAXING DAY OF SURFING -- HE LOOKS MORE TENSE THAN EVER!

STEP 3

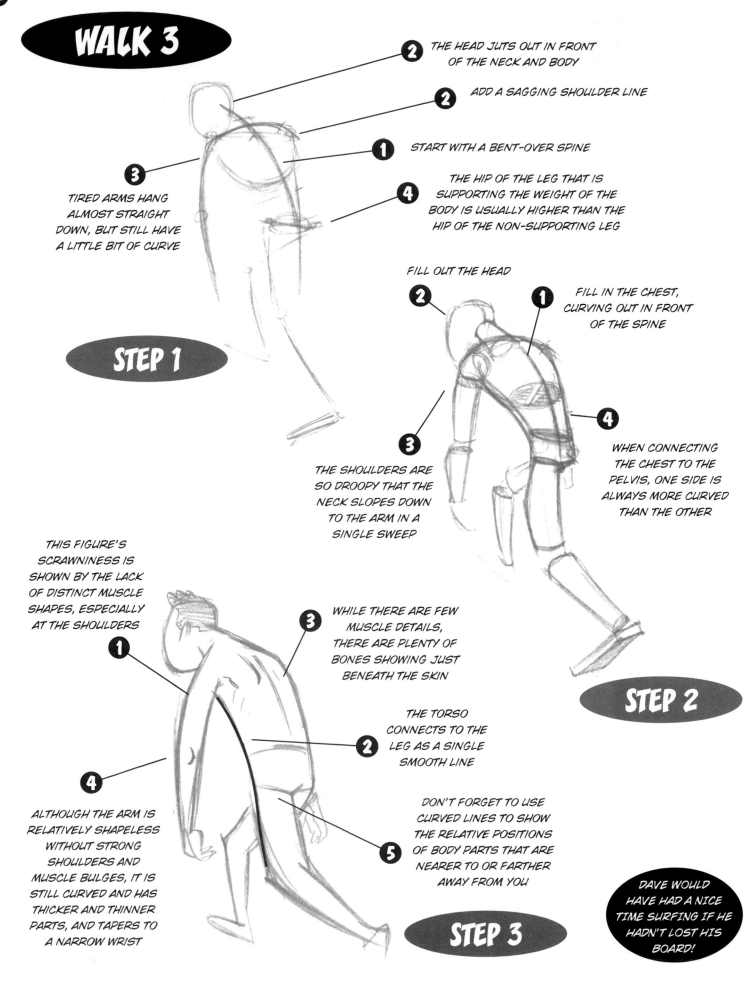

WALK 3

2 THE HEAD JUTS OUT IN FRONT OF THE NECK AND BODY

2 ADD A SAGGING SHOULDER LINE

1 START WITH A BENT-OVER SPINE

3 TIRED ARMS HANG ALMOST STRAIGHT DOWN, BUT STILL HAVE A LITTLE BIT OF CURVE

4 THE HIP OF THE LEG THAT IS SUPPORTING THE WEIGHT OF THE BODY IS USUALLY HIGHER THAN THE HIP OF THE NON-SUPPORTING LEG

STEP 1

FILL OUT THE HEAD

2

1 FILL IN THE CHEST, CURVING OUT IN FRONT OF THE SPINE

3 THE SHOULDERS ARE SO DROOPY THAT THE NECK SLOPES DOWN TO THE ARM IN A SINGLE SWEEP

4 WHEN CONNECTING THE CHEST TO THE PELVIS, ONE SIDE IS ALWAYS MORE CURVED THAN THE OTHER

STEP 2

THIS FIGURE'S SCRAWNINESS IS SHOWN BY THE LACK OF DISTINCT MUSCLE SHAPES, ESPECIALLY AT THE SHOULDERS

1

3 WHILE THERE ARE FEW MUSCLE DETAILS, THERE ARE PLENTY OF BONES SHOWING JUST BENEATH THE SKIN

2 THE TORSO CONNECTS TO THE LEG AS A SINGLE SMOOTH LINE

4 ALTHOUGH THE ARM IS RELATIVELY SHAPELESS WITHOUT STRONG SHOULDERS AND MUSCLE BULGES, IT IS STILL CURVED AND HAS THICKER AND THINNER PARTS, AND TAPERS TO A NARROW WRIST

5 DON'T FORGET TO USE CURVED LINES TO SHOW THE RELATIVE POSITIONS OF BODY PARTS THAT ARE NEARER TO OR FARTHER AWAY FROM YOU

STEP 3

DAVE WOULD HAVE HAD A NICE TIME SURFING IF HE HADN'T LOST HIS BOARD!

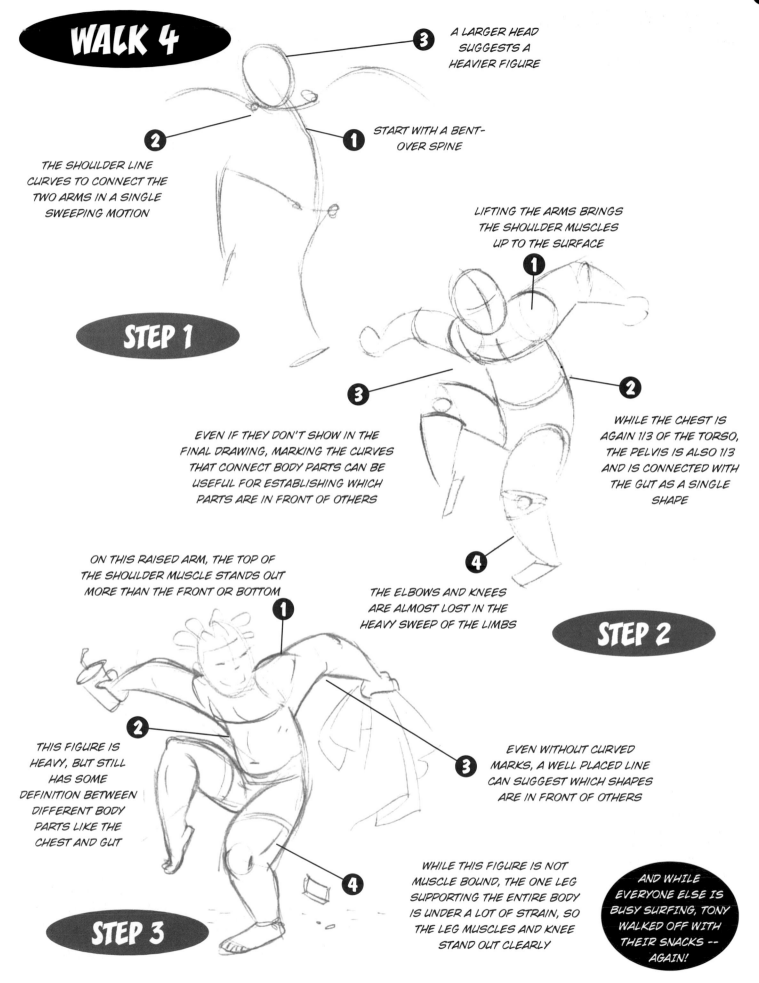

WALK 4

STEP 1

3 A LARGER HEAD SUGGESTS A HEAVIER FIGURE

1 START WITH A BENT-OVER SPINE

2 THE SHOULDER LINE CURVES TO CONNECT THE TWO ARMS IN A SINGLE SWEEPING MOTION

EVEN IF THEY DON'T SHOW IN THE FINAL DRAWING, MARKING THE CURVES THAT CONNECT BODY PARTS CAN BE USEFUL FOR ESTABLISHING WHICH PARTS ARE IN FRONT OF OTHERS

STEP 2

LIFTING THE ARMS BRINGS THE SHOULDER MUSCLES UP TO THE SURFACE

1

2 WHILE THE CHEST IS AGAIN 1/3 OF THE TORSO, THE PELVIS IS ALSO 1/3 AND IS CONNECTED WITH THE GUT AS A SINGLE SHAPE

3

4 THE ELBOWS AND KNEES ARE ALMOST LOST IN THE HEAVY SWEEP OF THE LIMBS

STEP 3

ON THIS RAISED ARM, THE TOP OF THE SHOULDER MUSCLE STANDS OUT MORE THAN THE FRONT OR BOTTOM

1

2 THIS FIGURE IS HEAVY, BUT STILL HAS SOME DEFINITION BETWEEN DIFFERENT BODY PARTS LIKE THE CHEST AND GUT

3 EVEN WITHOUT CURVED MARKS, A WELL PLACED LINE CAN SUGGEST WHICH SHAPES ARE IN FRONT OF OTHERS

4 WHILE THIS FIGURE IS NOT MUSCLE BOUND, THE ONE LEG SUPPORTING THE ENTIRE BODY IS UNDER A LOT OF STRAIN, SO THE LEG MUSCLES AND KNEE STAND OUT CLEARLY

AND WHILE EVERYONE ELSE IS BUSY SURFING, TONY WALKED OFF WITH THEIR SNACKS -- AGAIN!

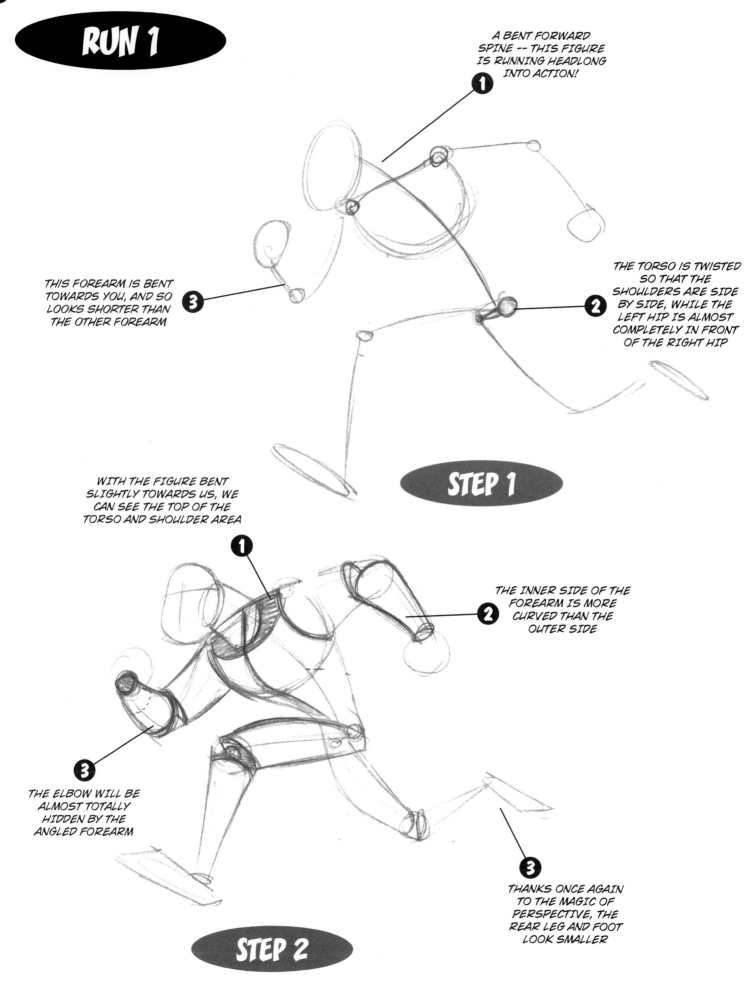

RUN 1

A BENT FORWARD SPINE -- THIS FIGURE IS RUNNING HEADLONG INTO ACTION!

1

THIS FOREARM IS BENT TOWARDS YOU, AND SO LOOKS SHORTER THAN THE OTHER FOREARM

3

THE TORSO IS TWISTED SO THAT THE SHOULDERS ARE SIDE BY SIDE, WHILE THE LEFT HIP IS ALMOST COMPLETELY IN FRONT OF THE RIGHT HIP

2

STEP 1

WITH THE FIGURE BENT SLIGHTLY TOWARDS US, WE CAN SEE THE TOP OF THE TORSO AND SHOULDER AREA

1

THE INNER SIDE OF THE FOREARM IS MORE CURVED THAN THE OUTER SIDE

2

THE ELBOW WILL BE ALMOST TOTALLY HIDDEN BY THE ANGLED FOREARM

3

THANKS ONCE AGAIN TO THE MAGIC OF PERSPECTIVE, THE REAR LEG AND FOOT LOOK SMALLER

3

STEP 2

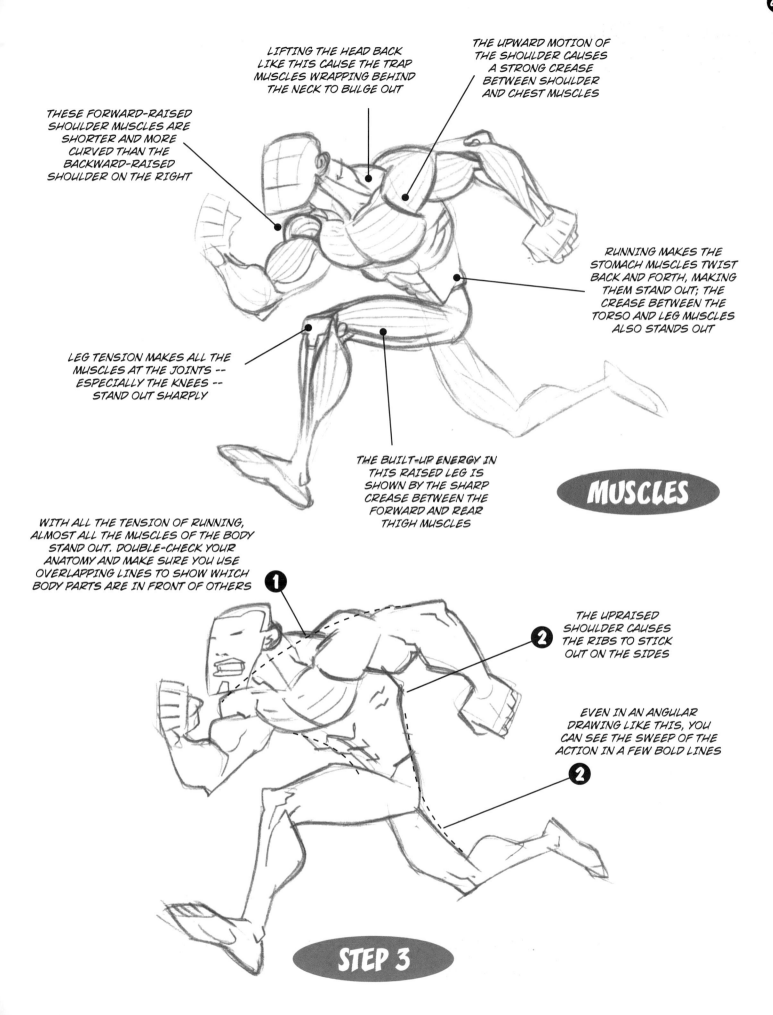

THESE FORWARD-RAISED SHOULDER MUSCLES ARE SHORTER AND MORE CURVED THAN THE BACKWARD-RAISED SHOULDER ON THE RIGHT

LIFTING THE HEAD BACK LIKE THIS CAUSE THE TRAP MUSCLES WRAPPING BEHIND THE NECK TO BULGE OUT

THE UPWARD MOTION OF THE SHOULDER CAUSES A STRONG CREASE BETWEEN SHOULDER AND CHEST MUSCLES

RUNNING MAKES THE STOMACH MUSCLES TWIST BACK AND FORTH, MAKING THEM STAND OUT; THE CREASE BETWEEN THE TORSO AND LEG MUSCLES ALSO STANDS OUT

LEG TENSION MAKES ALL THE MUSCLES AT THE JOINTS -- ESPECIALLY THE KNEES -- STAND OUT SHARPLY

THE BUILT-UP ENERGY IN THIS RAISED LEG IS SHOWN BY THE SHARP CREASE BETWEEN THE FORWARD AND REAR THIGH MUSCLES

MUSCLES

WITH ALL THE TENSION OF RUNNING, ALMOST ALL THE MUSCLES OF THE BODY STAND OUT. DOUBLE-CHECK YOUR ANATOMY AND MAKE SURE YOU USE OVERLAPPING LINES TO SHOW WHICH BODY PARTS ARE IN FRONT OF OTHERS

THE UPRAISED SHOULDER CAUSES THE RIBS TO STICK OUT ON THE SIDES

EVEN IN AN ANGULAR DRAWING LIKE THIS, YOU CAN SEE THE SWEEP OF THE ACTION IN A FEW BOLD LINES

STEP 3

RUN 2

START WITH AN UPRIGHT SPINE ①

THIS FOREARM IS BENT AWAY FROM YOU, AND SO LOOKS SHORTER THAN THE OTHER FOREARM ③

STEP 1

② **ONCE AGAIN, THE TORSO IS TWISTED, THIS TIME SO THAT ONE SHOULDER IS ALMOST COMPLETELY IN FRONT OF THE OTHER**

③ **THE LEGS FORM A LONG SWEEPING LINE**

③ **LIKE THE FOREARM, THIS PART OF THE LEG IS BENT AWAY AND FORESHORTENED**

AT THIS ANGLE, THE CURVES OF THE FOREARM ARE MORE PRONOUNCED ③

THIS TORSO IS ALMOST IN PROFILE, SO THE V-LINE IS OFF TO THE SIDE ①

STEP 2

② **THE FEMALE SHOULDER IS SMALLER, ABOUT 1/3 SIZE OF CHEST. THE SHOULDER CONNECTS THE ARM TO THE TORSO WITHOUT STICKING OUT TOO MUCH ON ITS OWN**

④ **EVEN WHEN LEGS ARE SPREAD THIS FAR APART, THE LEG/HIP SOCKETS ALWAYS CURVE INWARD**

SHARPEN THE SHOULDER TO EMPHASIZE THAT THE TORSO IS ARCHED BACK ①

REMEMBER TO USE OVERLAPPING LINES, ESPECIALLY WITH GROUPS OF FORESHORTENED SHAPES, TO CLARIFY WHICH SHAPES ARE IN FRONT OF OTHERS ②

AS ALWAYS, THE CURVES OF SOCKS AND OTHER CLOTHES HELP TO SHOW THE CURVES OF THE BODY ③

②

④ **THE FORWARD LEG IS CREASED WHERE IT MEETS THE HIP AT A SHARP ANGLE, THE REAR LEG HAS NO SHARP ANGLE AND NO CREASE**

STEP 3

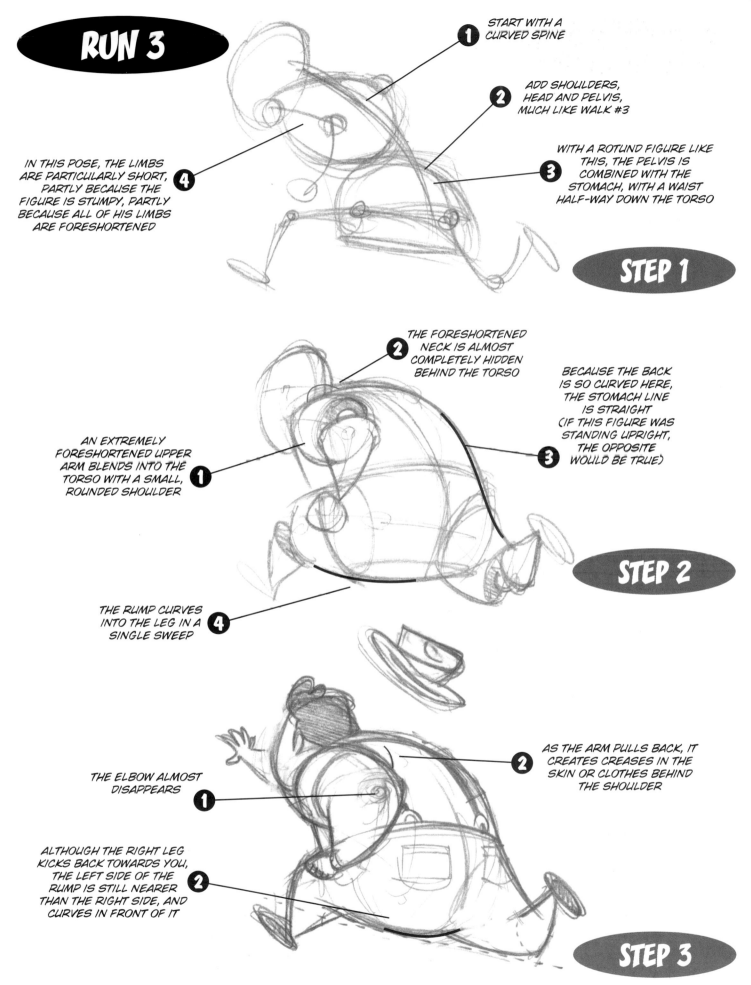

RUN 3

START WITH A CURVED SPINE

1

ADD SHOULDERS, HEAD AND PELVIS, MUCH LIKE WALK #3

2

WITH A ROTUND FIGURE LIKE THIS, THE PELVIS IS COMBINED WITH THE STOMACH, WITH A WAIST HALF-WAY DOWN THE TORSO

3

IN THIS POSE, THE LIMBS ARE PARTICULARLY SHORT, PARTLY BECAUSE THE FIGURE IS STUMPY, PARTLY BECAUSE ALL OF HIS LIMBS ARE FORESHORTENED

4

STEP 1

THE FORESHORTENED NECK IS ALMOST COMPLETELY HIDDEN BEHIND THE TORSO

2

BECAUSE THE BACK IS SO CURVED HERE, THE STOMACH LINE IS STRAIGHT (IF THIS FIGURE WAS STANDING UPRIGHT, THE OPPOSITE WOULD BE TRUE)

3

AN EXTREMELY FORESHORTENED UPPER ARM BLENDS INTO THE TORSO WITH A SMALL, ROUNDED SHOULDER

1

STEP 2

THE RUMP CURVES INTO THE LEG IN A SINGLE SWEEP

4

THE ELBOW ALMOST DISAPPEARS

1

AS THE ARM PULLS BACK, IT CREATES CREASES IN THE SKIN OR CLOTHES BEHIND THE SHOULDER

2

ALTHOUGH THE RIGHT LEG KICKS BACK TOWARDS YOU, THE LEFT SIDE OF THE RUMP IS STILL NEARER THAN THE RIGHT SIDE, AND CURVES IN FRONT OF IT

2

STEP 3

JUMP 1

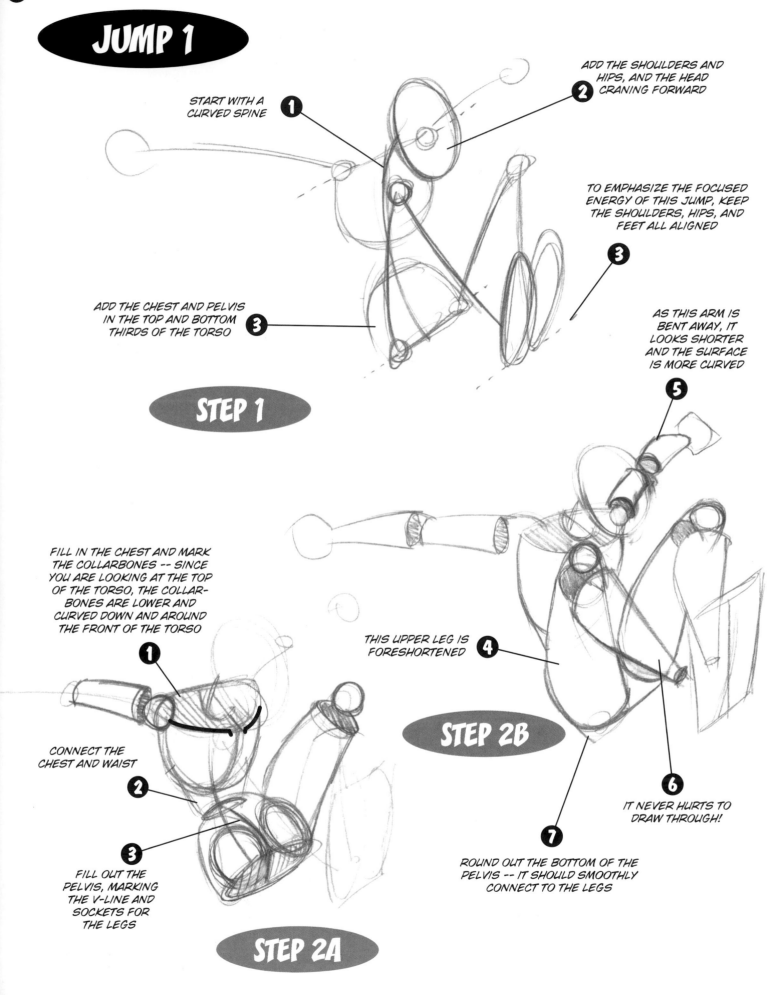

START WITH A CURVED SPINE **1**

2 ADD THE SHOULDERS AND HIPS, AND THE HEAD CRANING FORWARD

TO EMPHASIZE THE FOCUSED ENERGY OF THIS JUMP, KEEP THE SHOULDERS, HIPS, AND FEET ALL ALIGNED **3**

ADD THE CHEST AND PELVIS IN THE TOP AND BOTTOM THIRDS OF THE TORSO **3**

AS THIS ARM IS BENT AWAY, IT LOOKS SHORTER AND THE SURFACE IS MORE CURVED

STEP 1

FILL IN THE CHEST AND MARK THE COLLARBONES -- SINCE YOU ARE LOOKING AT THE TOP OF THE TORSO, THE COLLAR-BONES ARE LOWER AND CURVED DOWN AND AROUND THE FRONT OF THE TORSO **1**

5

THIS UPPER LEG IS FORESHORTENED **4**

CONNECT THE CHEST AND WAIST **2**

FILL OUT THE PELVIS, MARKING THE V-LINE AND SOCKETS FOR THE LEGS **3**

STEP 2B

6

7

IT NEVER HURTS TO DRAW THROUGH!

ROUND OUT THE BOTTOM OF THE PELVIS -- IT SHOULD SMOOTHLY CONNECT TO THE LEGS

STEP 2A

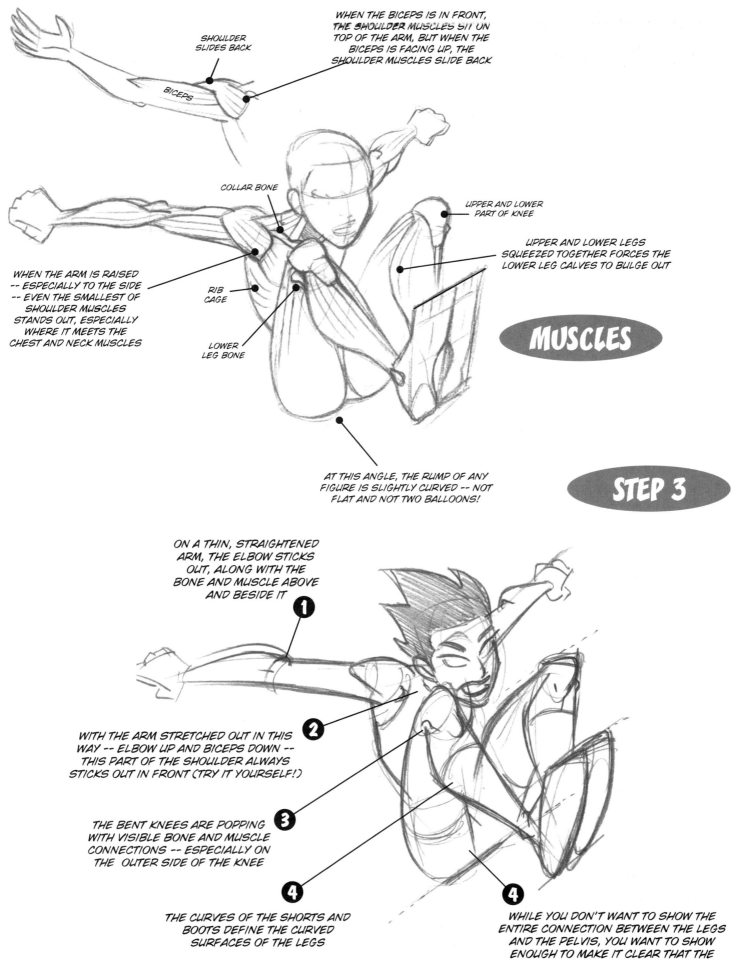

SHOULDER
SLIDES BACK

BICEPS

WHEN THE BICEPS IS IN FRONT,
THE SHOULDER MUSCLES SIT ON
TOP OF THE ARM, BUT WHEN THE
BICEPS IS FACING UP, THE
SHOULDER MUSCLES SLIDE BACK

COLLAR BONE

UPPER AND LOWER
PART OF KNEE

UPPER AND LOWER LEGS
SQUEEZED TOGETHER FORCES THE
LOWER LEG CALVES TO BULGE OUT

WHEN THE ARM IS RAISED
-- ESPECIALLY TO THE SIDE
-- EVEN THE SMALLEST OF
SHOULDER MUSCLES
STANDS OUT, ESPECIALLY
WHERE IT MEETS THE
CHEST AND NECK MUSCLES

RIB
CAGE

LOWER
LEG BONE

MUSCLES

AT THIS ANGLE, THE RUMP OF ANY
FIGURE IS SLIGHTLY CURVED -- NOT
FLAT AND NOT TWO BALLOONS!

STEP 3

ON A THIN, STRAIGHTENED
ARM, THE ELBOW STICKS
OUT, ALONG WITH THE
BONE AND MUSCLE ABOVE
AND BESIDE IT

1

WITH THE ARM STRETCHED OUT IN THIS
WAY -- ELBOW UP AND BICEPS DOWN --
THIS PART OF THE SHOULDER ALWAYS
STICKS OUT IN FRONT (TRY IT YOURSELF!)

2

THE BENT KNEES ARE POPPING
WITH VISIBLE BONE AND MUSCLE
CONNECTIONS -- ESPECIALLY ON
THE OUTER SIDE OF THE KNEE

3

4

THE CURVES OF THE SHORTS AND
BOOTS DEFINE THE CURVED
SURFACES OF THE LEGS

4

WHILE YOU DON'T WANT TO SHOW THE
ENTIRE CONNECTION BETWEEN THE LEGS
AND THE PELVIS, YOU WANT TO SHOW
ENOUGH TO MAKE IT CLEAR THAT THE
LEGS ARE BENT IN FRONT OF THE PELVIS

JUMP 2

STEP 1

2 ADD SHOULDERS AND HIPS, ALIGNED AS IN JUMP #1

4 WHEN LEGS ARE STRAIGHTENED OUT, THEY ACTUALLY CURVE SLIGHTLY BACKWARD

1 START WITH AN ARCHED SPINE

3 MARK OFF THE CHEST AND PELVIS

5 THE OUTSTRETCHED ARMS ARE ALSO SLIGHTLY CURVED

THE LEFT LEG LOOKS SHORTER THAN THE RIGHT -- THE TWO LEGS COME CLOSER TOGETHER AT THE FEET, SO THAT THE LEFT LEG IS AT A MORE FORESHORTENED ANGLE

4

3 DRAW THE V-LINE FOR THE BACK AND FRONT OF THE PELVIS, AND MARK THE TWO LEG SOCKETS, SO YOU CAN KEEP THE LEGS EQUAL LENGTH

1 FILL OUT THE TORSO

2 WHEN THE TORSO IS ARCHED BACK, THE RIBS STICK OUT MORE IN FRONT

5 THE ARMS AND SHOULDERS ARE LIFTED SO HIGH THAT THEY ARE ALMOST ON TOP OF THE TORSO. THIS ALSO CAUSES THE RIBS TO STICK OUT

HOW THE NECK CONNECTS TO THE BASE OF THE SKULL

STEP 2

3 ONLY DRAW ENOUGH OF AN OVERLAP TO SHOW THAT THE HIPS ARE IN FRONT OF THE LEGS

4 THE HIPS, KNEES, AND FEET ALL LINE UP

TAKE EXTRA CARE WITH COMPLEX AREAS WHERE SEVERAL MUSCLES AND BODY PARTS OVERLAP EACH OTHER

2 WHEN THE BACK IS ARCHED, THE SPINAL CREASE IS MORE OBVIOUS

1 THE FRONT AND BACK OF THE SHOULDER MUSCLE STAND OUT MORE CLEARLY AS SEPARATE PARTS WHEN THE SHOULDERS ARE RAISED, THE FRONT PORTION OF THE SHOULDER IS COMPRESSED WHILE THE BACK IS STRETCHED, AND THE CONNECTIONS BETWEEN THE SHOULDER, UPPER TORSO AND NECK STAND OUT CLEARLY

STEP 3

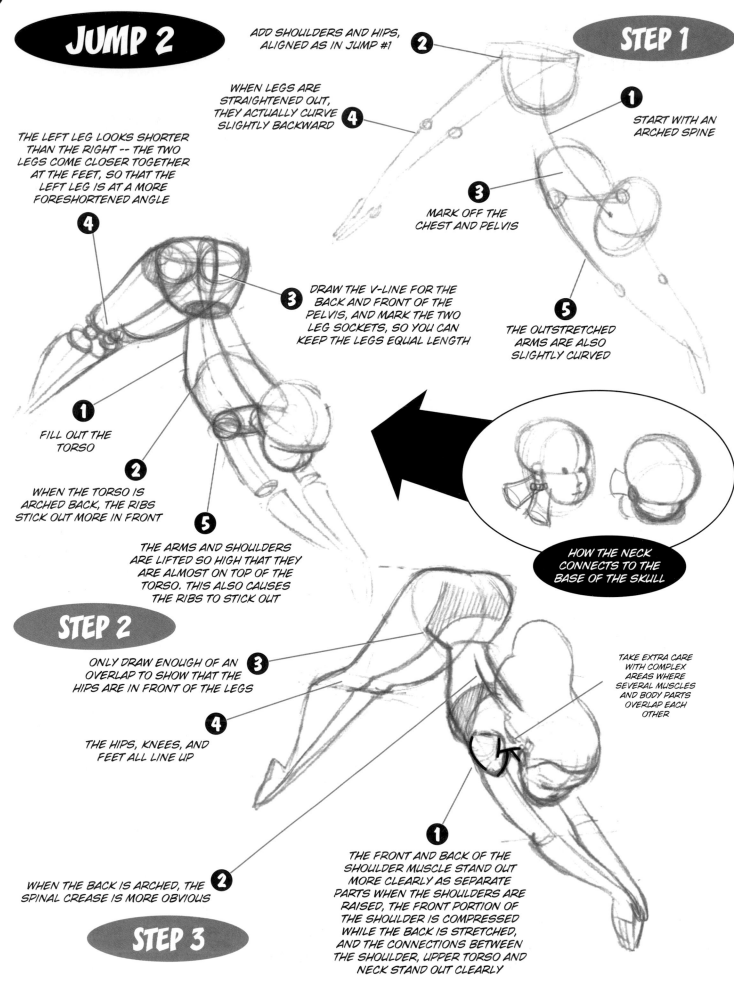

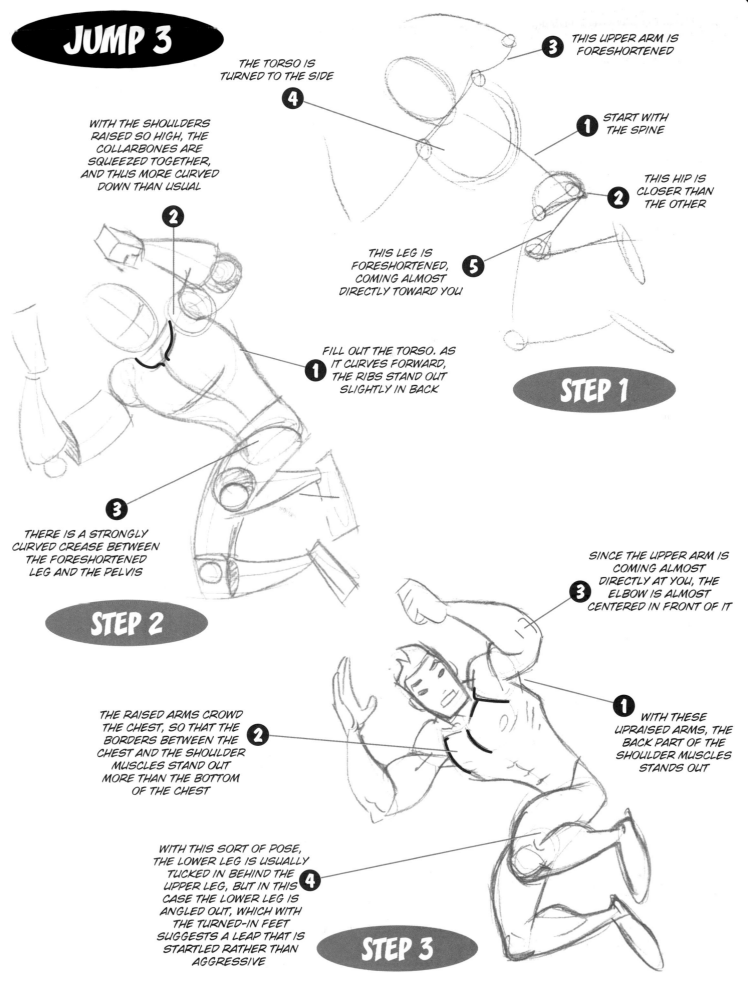

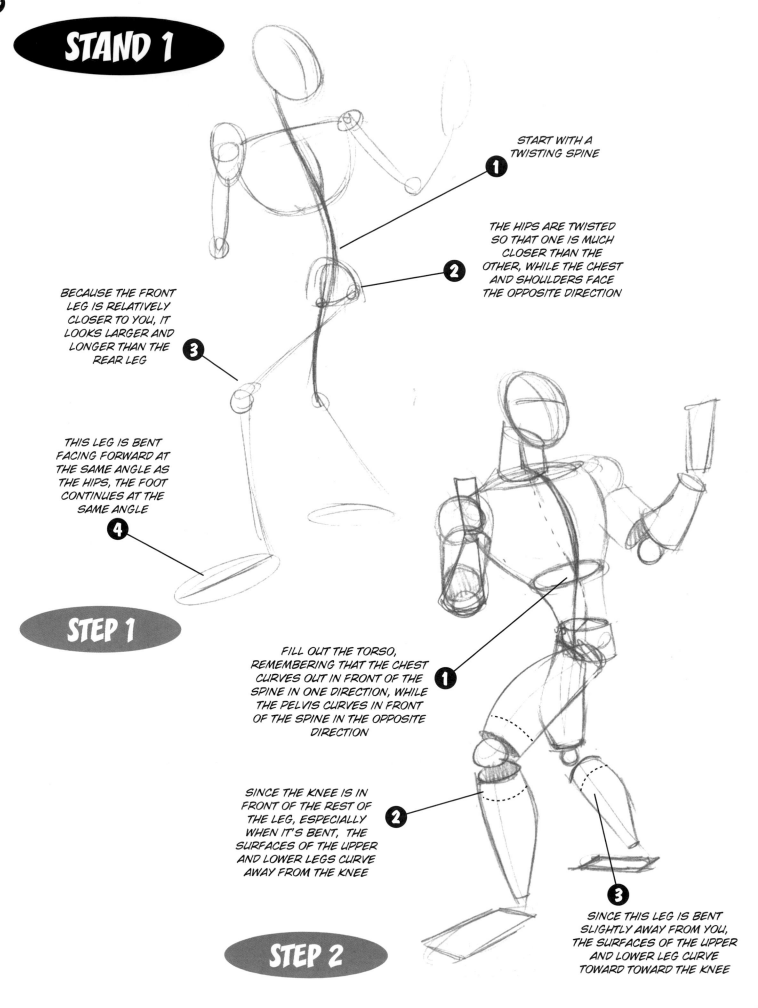

STAND 1

START WITH A TWISTING SPINE

1

THE HIPS ARE TWISTED SO THAT ONE IS MUCH CLOSER THAN THE OTHER, WHILE THE CHEST AND SHOULDERS FACE THE OPPOSITE DIRECTION

2

BECAUSE THE FRONT LEG IS RELATIVELY CLOSER TO YOU, IT LOOKS LARGER AND LONGER THAN THE REAR LEG

3

THIS LEG IS BENT FACING FORWARD AT THE SAME ANGLE AS THE HIPS, THE FOOT CONTINUES AT THE SAME ANGLE

4

STEP 1

FILL OUT THE TORSO, REMEMBERING THAT THE CHEST CURVES OUT IN FRONT OF THE SPINE IN ONE DIRECTION, WHILE THE PELVIS CURVES IN FRONT OF THE SPINE IN THE OPPOSITE DIRECTION

1

SINCE THE KNEE IS IN FRONT OF THE REST OF THE LEG, ESPECIALLY WHEN IT'S BENT, THE SURFACES OF THE UPPER AND LOWER LEGS CURVE AWAY FROM THE KNEE

2

3

SINCE THIS LEG IS BENT SLIGHTLY AWAY FROM YOU, THE SURFACES OF THE UPPER AND LOWER LEG CURVE TOWARD TOWARD THE KNEE

STEP 2

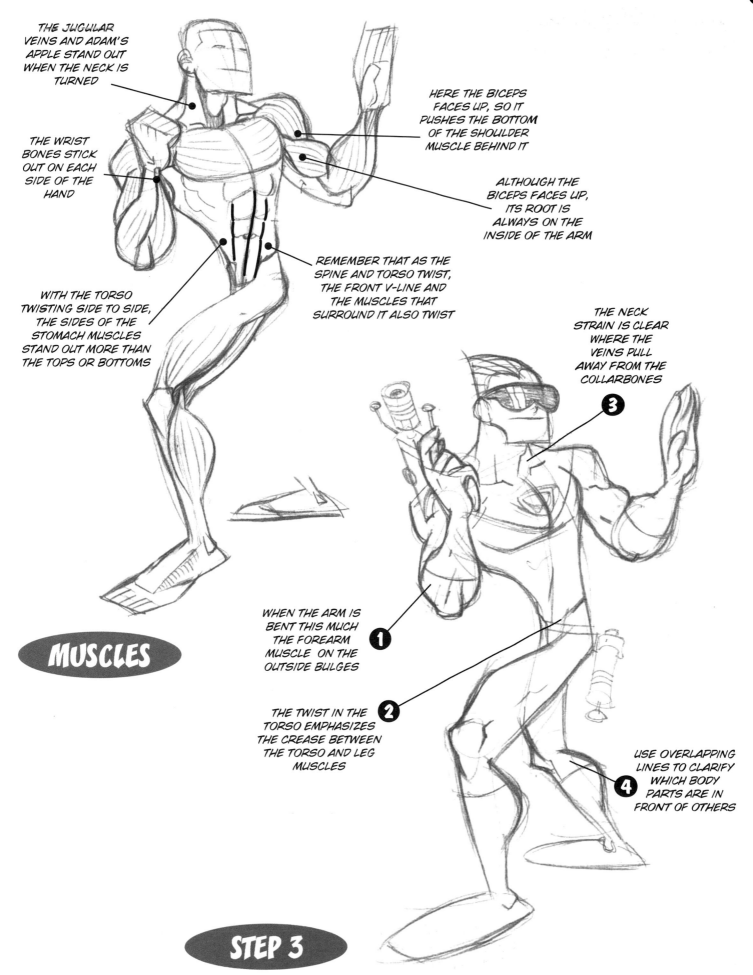

THE JUGULAR VEINS AND ADAM'S APPLE STAND OUT WHEN THE NECK IS TURNED

THE WRIST BONES STICK OUT ON EACH SIDE OF THE HAND

WITH THE TORSO TWISTING SIDE TO SIDE, THE SIDES OF THE STOMACH MUSCLES STAND OUT MORE THAN THE TOPS OR BOTTOMS

HERE THE BICEPS FACES UP, SO IT PUSHES THE BOTTOM OF THE SHOULDER MUSCLE BEHIND IT

ALTHOUGH THE BICEPS FACES UP, ITS ROOT IS ALWAYS ON THE INSIDE OF THE ARM

REMEMBER THAT AS THE SPINE AND TORSO TWIST, THE FRONT V-LINE AND THE MUSCLES THAT SURROUND IT ALSO TWIST

THE NECK STRAIN IS CLEAR WHERE THE VEINS PULL AWAY FROM THE COLLARBONES

WHEN THE ARM IS BENT THIS MUCH THE FOREARM MUSCLE ON THE OUTSIDE BULGES

THE TWIST IN THE TORSO EMPHASIZES THE CREASE BETWEEN THE TORSO AND LEG MUSCLES

USE OVERLAPPING LINES TO CLARIFY WHICH BODY PARTS ARE IN FRONT OF OTHERS

MUSCLES

STEP 3

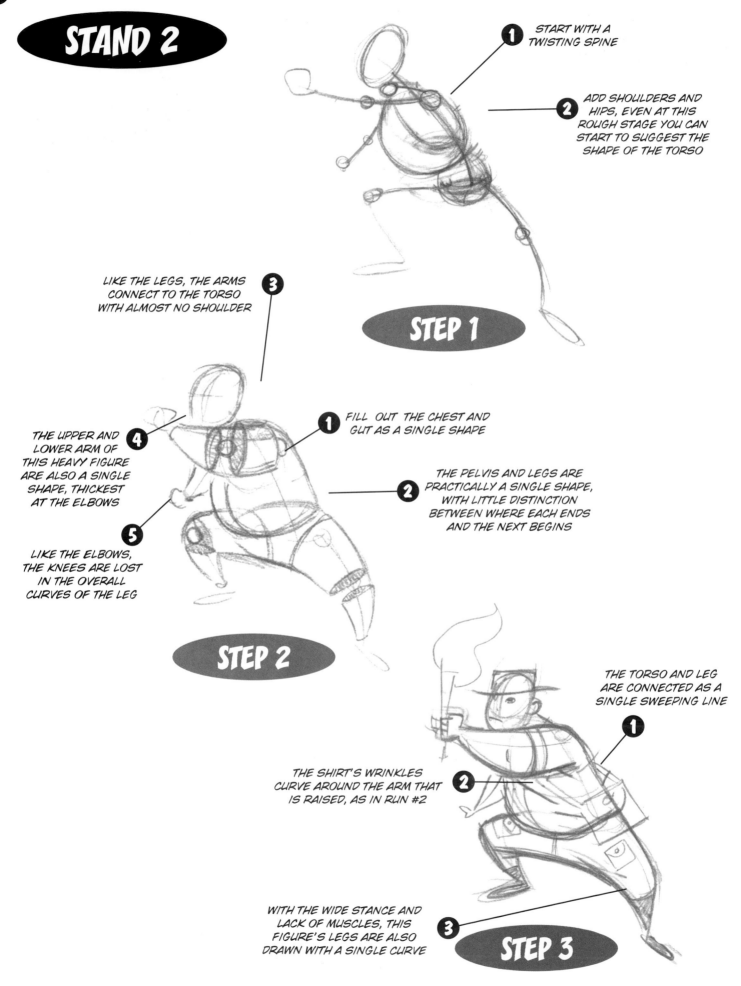

STAND 2

1 START WITH A TWISTING SPINE

2 ADD SHOULDERS AND HIPS, EVEN AT THIS ROUGH STAGE YOU CAN START TO SUGGEST THE SHAPE OF THE TORSO

STEP 1

3 LIKE THE LEGS, THE ARMS CONNECT TO THE TORSO WITH ALMOST NO SHOULDER

4 THE UPPER AND LOWER ARM OF THIS HEAVY FIGURE ARE ALSO A SINGLE SHAPE, THICKEST AT THE ELBOWS

5 LIKE THE ELBOWS, THE KNEES ARE LOST IN THE OVERALL CURVES OF THE LEG

1 FILL OUT THE CHEST AND GUT AS A SINGLE SHAPE

2 THE PELVIS AND LEGS ARE PRACTICALLY A SINGLE SHAPE, WITH LITTLE DISTINCTION BETWEEN WHERE EACH ENDS AND THE NEXT BEGINS

STEP 2

1 THE TORSO AND LEG ARE CONNECTED AS A SINGLE SWEEPING LINE

2 THE SHIRT'S WRINKLES CURVE AROUND THE ARM THAT IS RAISED, AS IN RUN #2

3 WITH THE WIDE STANCE AND LACK OF MUSCLES, THIS FIGURE'S LEGS ARE ALSO DRAWN WITH A SINGLE CURVE

STEP 3

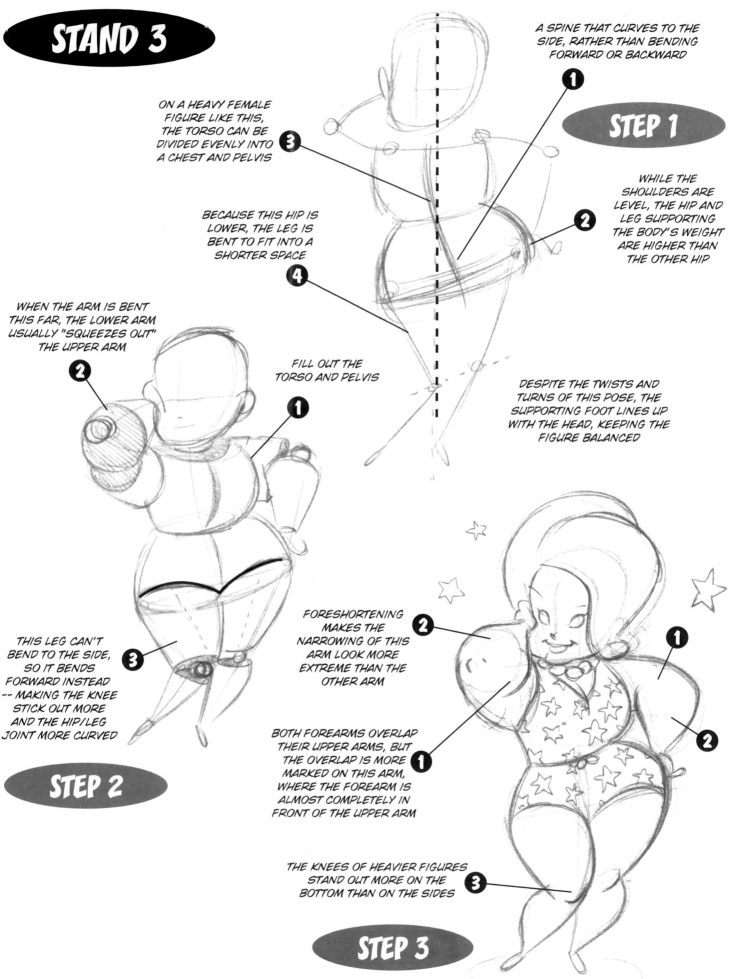

STAND 4

THERE'S VERY LITTLE NEW IN THE FOLLOWING TWO POSES -- JUST A CHANCE TO USE WHAT YOU'VE SEEN IN EARLIER POSES

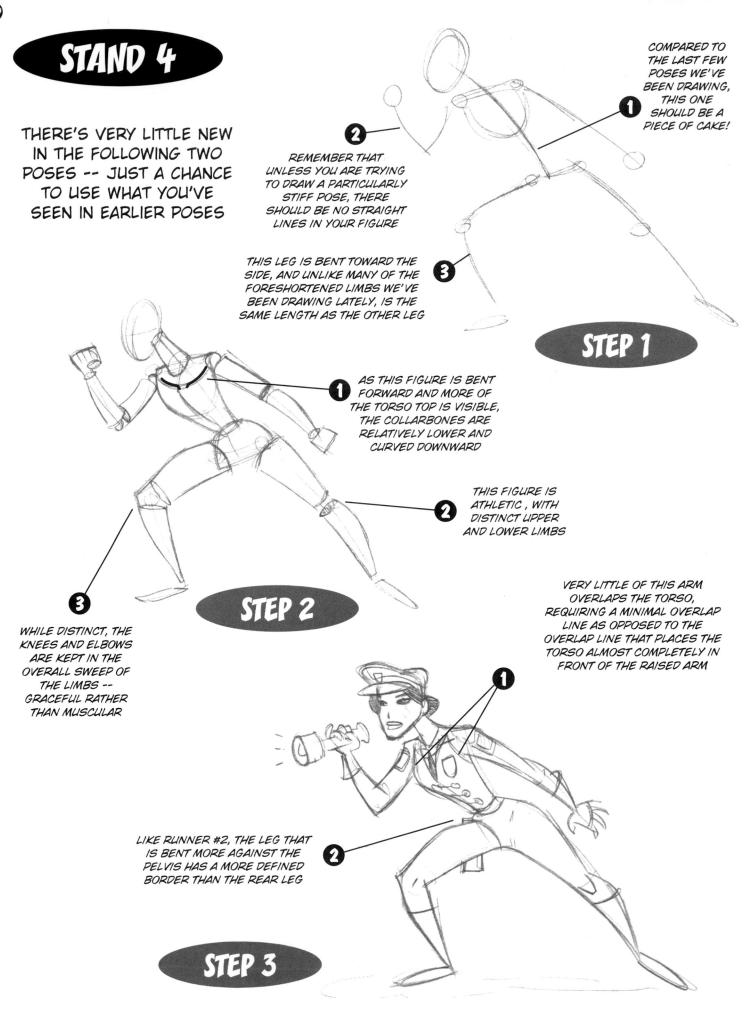

COMPARED TO THE LAST FEW POSES WE'VE BEEN DRAWING, THIS ONE SHOULD BE A PIECE OF CAKE!

2 REMEMBER THAT UNLESS YOU ARE TRYING TO DRAW A PARTICULARLY STIFF POSE, THERE SHOULD BE NO STRAIGHT LINES IN YOUR FIGURE

3 THIS LEG IS BENT TOWARD THE SIDE, AND UNLIKE MANY OF THE FORESHORTENED LIMBS WE'VE BEEN DRAWING LATELY, IS THE SAME LENGTH AS THE OTHER LEG

STEP 1

1 AS THIS FIGURE IS BENT FORWARD AND MORE OF THE TORSO TOP IS VISIBLE, THE COLLARBONES ARE RELATIVELY LOWER AND CURVED DOWNWARD

2 THIS FIGURE IS ATHLETIC, WITH DISTINCT UPPER AND LOWER LIMBS

3 WHILE DISTINCT, THE KNEES AND ELBOWS ARE KEPT IN THE OVERALL SWEEP OF THE LIMBS -- GRACEFUL RATHER THAN MUSCULAR

STEP 2

VERY LITTLE OF THIS ARM OVERLAPS THE TORSO, REQUIRING A MINIMAL OVERLAP LINE AS OPPOSED TO THE OVERLAP LINE THAT PLACES THE TORSO ALMOST COMPLETELY IN FRONT OF THE RAISED ARM

1

2 LIKE RUNNER #2, THE LEG THAT IS BENT MORE AGAINST THE PELVIS HAS A MORE DEFINED BORDER THAN THE REAR LEG

STEP 3

STAND 5

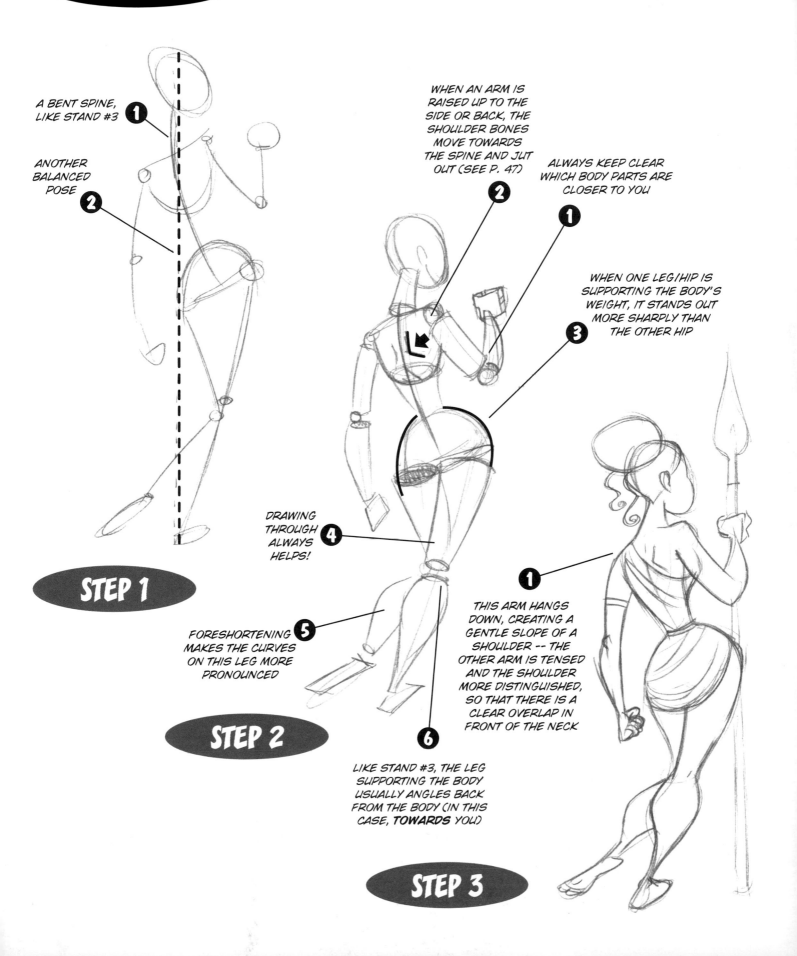

A BENT SPINE, LIKE STAND #3 ❶

ANOTHER BALANCED POSE ❷

STEP 1

WHEN AN ARM IS RAISED UP TO THE SIDE OR BACK, THE SHOULDER BONES MOVE TOWARDS THE SPINE AND JUT OUT (SEE P. 47) ❷

ALWAYS KEEP CLEAR WHICH BODY PARTS ARE CLOSER TO YOU ❶

WHEN ONE LEG/HIP IS SUPPORTING THE BODY'S WEIGHT, IT STANDS OUT MORE SHARPLY THAN THE OTHER HIP ❸

DRAWING THROUGH ALWAYS HELPS! ❹

FORESHORTENING MAKES THE CURVES ON THIS LEG MORE PRONOUNCED ❺

STEP 2

THIS ARM HANGS DOWN, CREATING A GENTLE SLOPE OF A SHOULDER -- THE OTHER ARM IS TENSED AND THE SHOULDER MORE DISTINGUISHED, SO THAT THERE IS A CLEAR OVERLAP IN FRONT OF THE NECK ❶

LIKE STAND #3, THE LEG SUPPORTING THE BODY USUALLY ANGLES BACK FROM THE BODY (IN THIS CASE, **TOWARDS** YOU) ❻

STEP 3

PUNCH 1

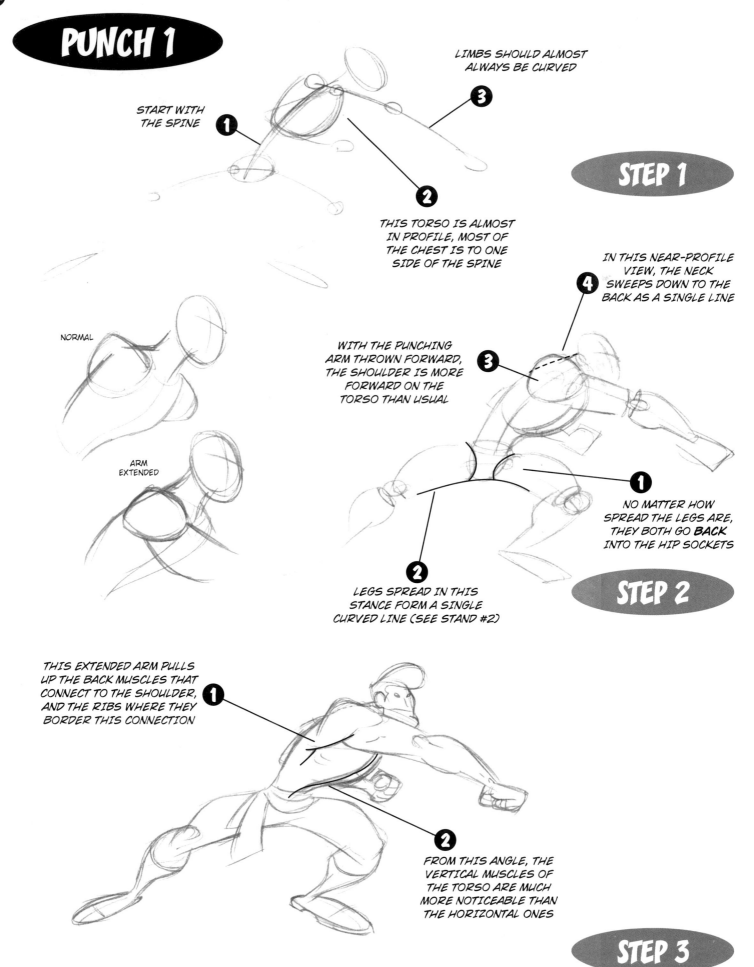

LIMBS SHOULD ALMOST ALWAYS BE CURVED

3

START WITH THE SPINE

1

2

STEP 1

THIS TORSO IS ALMOST IN PROFILE, MOST OF THE CHEST IS TO ONE SIDE OF THE SPINE

IN THIS NEAR-PROFILE VIEW, THE NECK SWEEPS DOWN TO THE BACK AS A SINGLE LINE

4

NORMAL

WITH THE PUNCHING ARM THROWN FORWARD, THE SHOULDER IS MORE FORWARD ON THE TORSO THAN USUAL

3

ARM EXTENDED

1

NO MATTER HOW SPREAD THE LEGS ARE, THEY BOTH GO **BACK** INTO THE HIP SOCKETS

2

LEGS SPREAD IN THIS STANCE FORM A SINGLE CURVED LINE (SEE STAND #2)

STEP 2

THIS EXTENDED ARM PULLS UP THE BACK MUSCLES THAT CONNECT TO THE SHOULDER, AND THE RIBS WHERE THEY BORDER THIS CONNECTION

1

2

FROM THIS ANGLE, THE VERTICAL MUSCLES OF THE TORSO ARE MUCH MORE NOTICEABLE THAN THE HORIZONTAL ONES

STEP 3

PUNCH 2

OKAY... SO THAT LAST ONE WAS EASY, RIGHT? NOW TRY YOUR HAND AT SOME HEAVY-DUTY FORESHORTENING!

STEP 1

3 FORESHORTENED FOREARM

1 START WITH THE SPINE

2 WITH BOTH ARMS RAISED, THE SHOULDER LINE CURVES UP TO THE SHOULDERS

STEP 2

1 THE CURVES ON THE FORESHORTENED ARM ARE MORE EXTREME THAN THOSE OF THE OTHER ARM

2 ANOTHER CONTINUOUS LINE

STEP 3

1 THE TWIST AND STRAIN OF THE NECK MAKES THE ADAM'S APPLE STAND OUT, AS WELL AS THE CONNECTION BETWEEN THE JUGULAR VEINS AND THE COLLARBONES

2 BECAUSE THE SHOULDERS ARE RAISED, THE TRAP MUSCLES BULGE OUT, BUT ARE DISTINCT FROM THE SQUARED-OFF SHAPE OF THE TWO SHOULDERS

5 THE CURVING JOINT BETWEEN THE FOREARM AND UPPER ARM IS SO MARKED BECAUSE THE FOREARM IS FORESHORTENED **AND** THE TWO PARTS OF THE ARM ARE PRESSED TOGETHER, MAKING A CREASE

6 THE TWISTING TORSO EMPHASIZES THE BORDER BETWEEN THE TORSO AND THE LEG MUSCLES

3 THE SHOULDER/CHEST BORDER STANDS OUT

4 WHEN A BODY PART IS FORESHORTENED TO THIS EXTREME, THE SURFACE CURVES ALMOST SHOW "CROSS SECTIONS" OF THE WRIST, ELBOW, TRICEPS, AND SHOULDER

7 WITH THE RAISED ARM AND FORWARD-LEANING TORSO, THE SIDE RIBS STAND OUT

PRACTICE POSES

SO NOW YOU'VE SEEN IT DONE STEP-BY-STEP... IT'S YOUR TURN! HERE ARE A HANDFUL OF ACTION SKELETONS AND FINISHED DRAWINGS, WITH NO EDUCATIONAL CHATTER TO DISTRACT YOU. SEE IF YOU REMEMBER ALL THE TRICKS OF MUSCLES, FORESHORTENING, AND LINES!

PUNCH

KICK

HUNT

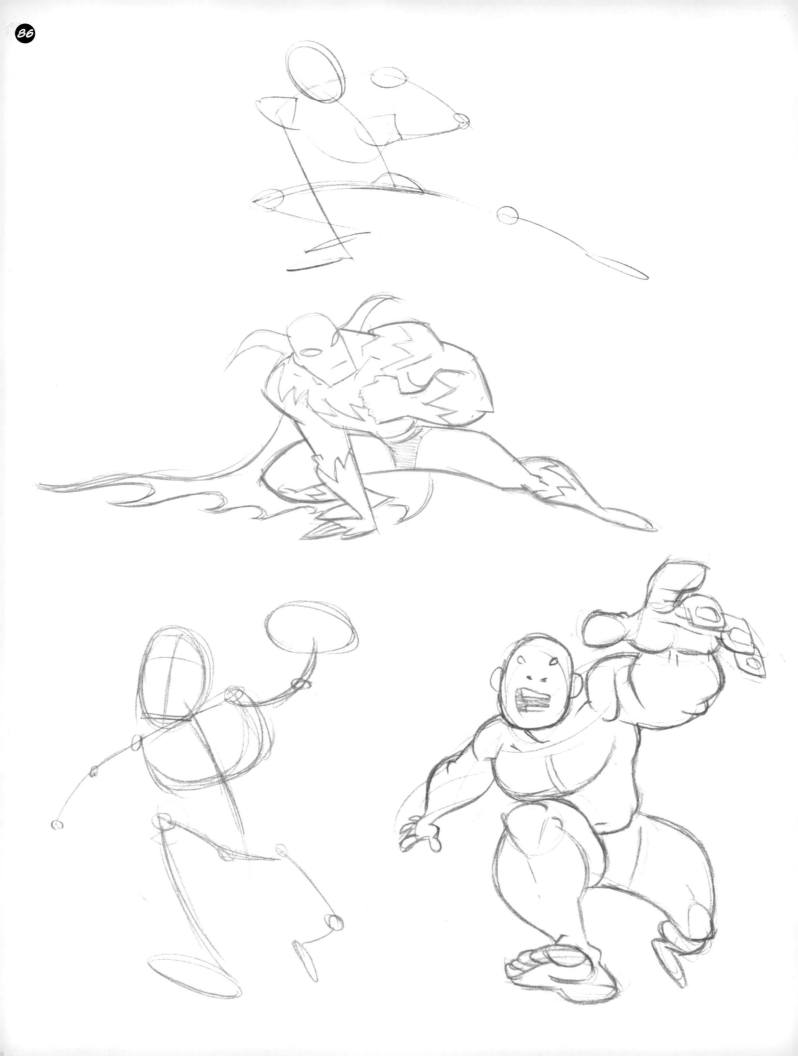

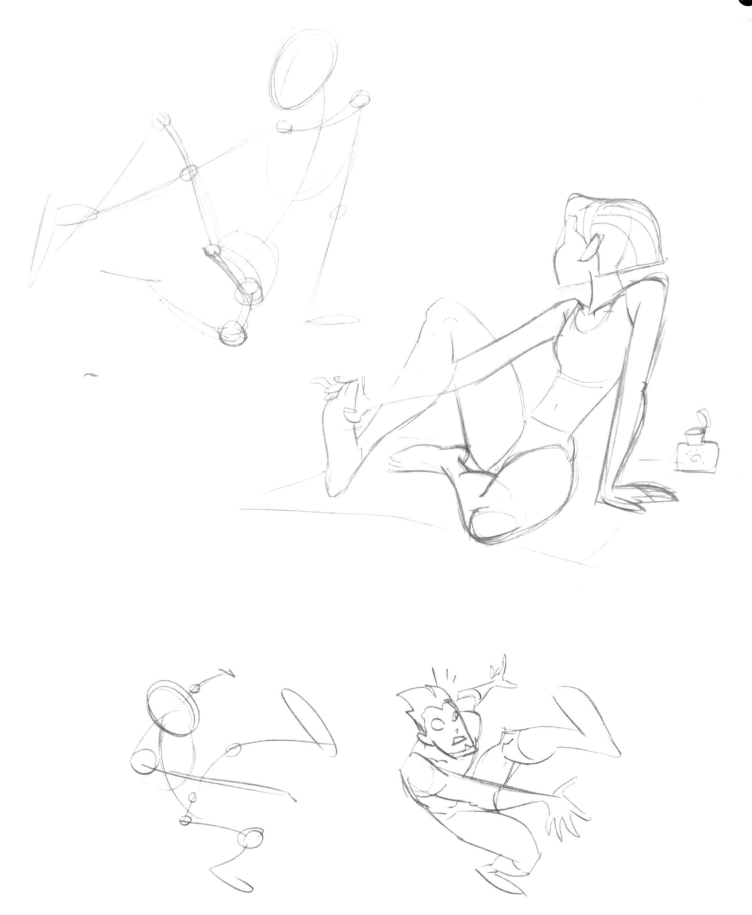

IF YOU'VE DRAWN ALL THESE FIGURES ONCE, WHY NOT DRAW THEM AGAIN? ONLY THIS TIME, CHANGE THEIR FACE OR BODY TYPES, OR MOVE THE LIMBS AROUND A LITTLE... THERE'S NOTHING LIKE VARIETY!

STYLES

OF COURSE, THESE ARE ONLY A FEW
EXAMPLES OF THE MILLIONS OF STYLES
OF CARTOONING YOU CAN PLAY WITH.

INDEX